NINETEENTH-CENTURY INVENTORS

AMERICAN PROFILES

NINETEENTH-CENTURY INVENTORS

■

Jon Noonan

Facts On File
New York • Oxford

Nineteenth-Century Inventors

Facts On File, Inc.
460 Park Avenue South
New York NY 10016
USA

Facts On File Limited
Collins Street
Oxford OX4 1XJ
United Kingdom

Library of Congress Cataloging-in-Publication Data
Noonan, Jon.
Nineteenth-century inventors / Jon Noonan.
p.   cm. — (American profiles)
Includes bibliographical references and index.
Summary: Describes the lives and achievements of eight of the most
   important inventors of the nineteenth century, including Edison,
   Fulton, Hollerith, and McCormick.
ISBN 0-8160-2480-4
1. Inventors—United States—Biography—Juvenile literature.
2. Inventions—United States—History—19th century—Juvenile
literature. [1. Inventors. 2. Inventions.] I. Title
II. Title: 19th-century inventors. III. Series: American profiles
(Facts On File, Inc.)
T39.N66   1992
609'.2'273—dc20
[B]   91-13584

A British CIP catalogue record for this book is available from the British Library.

Facts On File books are available at special discounts when purchased in bulk quantities for businesses, associations, institutions or sales promotions. Please call our Special Sales Department in New York at 212/683-2244 (dial 800/322-8755 except in NY, AK, or HI) or in Oxford at 865/728399.

Text design by Ron Monteleone
Jacket design by Ron Monteleone
Composition by Facts On File, Inc.
Manufactured by The Maple-Vail Book Manufacturing Group
Printed in the United States of America

10 9 8 7 6 5 4 3 2 1

*To all good teachers, writers, editors, librarians, students,
and inventors everywhere, and especially to
my lovely, intelligent, and supportive wife
Susan and my children
Kenneth and Clarissa,
with love*

The right of an inventor to his invention is a natural right, which existed before the Constitution was written and which is above the Constitution.

—Daniel Webster

Contents

Acknowledgments

I would like to thank the libraries, museums, and companies that provided information and materials for this book, especially the Library of Congress, the Smithsonian Institution, the Edison National Historic Site, the Goodyear Tire and Rubber Company, Westinghouse Electric Corporation, and International Business Machines. In particular, I would like to express thanks to Randolph Hershey, Barbara Henninger, George Tselos, and Charles A. Ruch for their efficient services.

Introduction

*O*ne of the most favorable times to be an inventor began in America soon after the Constitution was signed in 1787. Continuing into the 1800s, the environment for inventors improved even more.

Under the Constitution, Congress was given the power "to promote the progress of science and useful arts, by securing for limited times to authors and inventors the exclusive right to their respective writings and discoveries."

The first session of Congress was held in 1789. In that same year, George Washington began his term as the first president of the United States. As his secretary of state, Washington chose Thomas Jefferson.

George Washington and Thomas Jefferson were inventors. Among their inventions were new plows by Washington as well as an adjustable writing desk and swivel chair by Jefferson.

The enthusiasm for inventions in the new country led Congress to pass the Patent Act of 1790. It was hoped that inventors would be attracted to the idea of getting credit for their creations and that the number of inventions would grow in the future.

A license called a patent, would be given for each invention, granting the inventor the exclusive right to make, sell, or profit from it for a certain number of years. The approval of patents was to be handled by the secretary of state and two other members of George Washington's cabinet. As soon as these cabinet members took charge of their new assignment, applications started to arrive. Jefferson said, "The issue of patents for new discoveries has given a spring to invention beyond my conception."

Also in 1790, Congress passed the Census Act, calling for a census to be conducted under the supervision of the secretary of state in accordance with Section 2 of Article 1 of the Constitution, which states that the population of each state in the country is to be counted every 10 years. For each decade of the 1800s, the census gave information on the swift growth of the country. The numbers provided inventors an incentive to satisfy the needs of an expanding and changing nation.

The census of 1800 put the United States population at 5.3 million in a land of 865,000 square miles. By 1850, the census counted over 23 million people in a country of 2,993,000 square miles. By the end of the century, the population had grown beyond 75 million.

The United States has always been a country of change. This condition became evident as early as the term of Thomas Jefferson, who became president in 1801. During his first term of office, Jefferson approved the Louisiana Purchase in 1803. This land, obtained from France, more than doubled the size of the country, setting the stage for a century of growth.

Elected to a second term, Jefferson signed the law that forbade further importation of slaves into the United States effective on January 1, 1808. By this action, Jefferson and the Congress continued the trend toward creating a country where everyone would be entitled to "life, liberty, and the pursuit of happiness," the words that had been chosen by Jefferson himself for the Declaration of Independence in 1776. Several states had already abolished slavery by 1808. Before the end of the century, slavery would be abolished throughout the country.

On the inside wall of the Jefferson Memorial in Washington, D.C., some of the thoughts that Thomas Jefferson expressed about change can be read. He noted that as the human mind "becomes more developed, more enlightened, as new discoveries are made [and] new truths discovered . . . institutions must advance also to keep pace with the times."

Jefferson's second term as the president of the United States ended in 1809. By this time, new generations of inventors had come along to further the legacy of liberty left by the Founding Fathers. Robert Fulton was full-grown, Samuel Morse was a teenager, Charles Goodyear was a child, and Cyrus Hall McCormick was just about to be born.

As great as Jefferson's changes were, greater ones were still to come. New inventions would eventually cause old ideas of conquest and control to crumble. Good inventions became the key to a better future.

That the control of large amounts of land would bring increased prosperity was becoming an outdated idea. Inventions would soon create greater wealth than large land holdings alone could provide. In the future, countries could enjoy high standards of living regardless of their size. Wealth would flow to the countries with the best inventions.

Introduction

Slavery became an old idea when new equipment could perform the work better and more cheaply. Soon, one machine could handle the work of a hundred laborers in the field, and new appliances would free servants from the home. To complete a task, the touch of a button replaced long hours of toil.

That transportation had to be slow; that every person on the planet had to be a farmer or hunter in order to eat, unless they were privileged; that no new materials could ever be formed; that only fire could illumine the night; that no one could talk to a person on the other side of the world; that nature's power could never come cheaply; that no one could ever count faster than their brains allowed—these ideas and more soon crumbled and vanished.

The inventors in this book were part of this process. They, and others like them, changed the world. Their efforts created new tools and changed the transportation, communication, agricultural, computational, and energy systems of the earth.

In the early 1800s, America was still a nation of farmers. Hand implements, virtually unchanged for centuries, were the only tools available for harvesting crops. The most common forms of travel were walking or being carried by horse or boat. Relative to the future, communication was slow and so was change.

Then came the steamboat, farming machinery, the telegraph, and synthetic materials. About the same time, the railroads appeared. In 1830, there were only 23 miles of usable track in the United States, but that was soon to change. By 1850, there were 5,000 miles of track and 20 years later, 75,000 miles. Steamboats increased in size and number; new farming equipment filled the country with food; the telegraph lines grew alongside the expanding railroads; and a thousand uses were found for vulcanized rubber and other new materials.

Then the next generation of inventors came along. By the end of the Civil War in 1865, Thomas Edison, George Westinghouse, and Alexander Graham Bell were teenagers. Herman Hollerith was a child. Inspired by the inventions they saw around them, they proceeded to devise some of their own.

By the end of the century, there were over 200,000 miles of railroad track. America had phonographs, electric lights, transportation safety devices, giant electric generating stations, telephones, fast-moving data processing machines, and many more new inventions.

The inventors in this book shared several common attributes. They were inspired by the prospects of success that awaited those who created something significant. They achieved their success in America, where they made full use of the advantages available to them. These inventors all experienced suffering as children, shared a faith in God, developed a strong try-again attitude, and held fast to the idea that someday they would achieve greatness.

America provided some of the essential ingredients these inventors needed to ensure success. First among those was freedom. Without the freedom to create, they could not have realized their inventions. Liberty was guaranteed by the Constitution and the Bill of Rights.

Income was a second incentive. The fact for these individuals was that if there had been no hope of monetary reward, they would not have turned to inventing. There was no income tax in 19th-century America. All these inventors hoped to earn a good living through their inventions.

Protection was a third concern. The Constitution and the Patent Acts of 1790 and 1793 provided the first level. It was improved with the Patent Act of 1836. Just as Jefferson recommended, institutions had to change to keep pace with new circumstances. Before 1836, hundreds of inventors filed applications for similar inventions. With the new law, only new and useful inventions would receive a patent. From then on, all patents were given a separate number, as well, instead of being filed by name.

The other ingredients for success were supplied by the inventors themselves. Their stories are found in the chapters that follow.

These inventors gave impetus to the technological age. They, and a few others before them, were the first source of inspiration for inventors in the current century. They were the source from which future inventions flowed.

Like these inventors, the inventors of the future face great challenges. Their solutions can be just as fantastic. They will thrive, given an environment of freedom. They will expand their knowledge of how things work, grow stronger than their fears and afflictions, and learn to ignore the negative comments of others. Through constant improvement, the day may come when their efforts, too, will be successful. Then new stories will be written about these select individuals so that the *next* generation of inventors can read about *them*. The process of change will continue.

NINETEENTH-CENTURY INVENTORS

Robert Fulton
(1765–1815)

*Robert Fulton engraving; copied originally from
a portrait painted by Benjamin West in 1806.*
(National Archives)

Although Robert Fulton is best known for his steamboat, commonly called the *Clermont*, which was first launched in 1807 and was the first steamboat to be a commercial success, there is another important invention credited to him.

In the summer of 1801, in the seaport of Brest on the Atlantic coast of France, the original *Nautilus* submarine, the first of its kind, just over 20 feet long and five feet wide, floated ready for testing. Its inventor and captain, Fulton, gave the command, and, with a crew of three men, the *Nautilus* submerged to 25 feet below the surface of the ocean. Sea-filtered light streamed through a

1

one-and-a-half-inch window in the top of the submarine. Sitting by the light, Fulton counted the time ticking by on his timepiece.

With the help of a compressed air supply, Fulton and his crew stayed underwater for over four hours. After surfacing, they raised the folded mast and sailed the *Nautilus* across the sea. Then they folded their sail, refilled their ballast tank with seawater, and submerged again. They traveled 400 meters, hand turning the crank that spun their propeller. They also steered to their port and starboard sides (left and right). Then they rose to the surface, looked around, submerged again, and returned to where they started. Fulton said they had completed every essential test. However, it was not this submarine, but the steamboat, that was to bring Fulton his fame.

On November 14, 1765, Robert Fulton was born in a stone farmhouse in southern Pennsylvania. He had three older sisters, Betsy, Bell, and Polly, and was soon followed by a younger brother, Abraham.

There is little record of Fulton's boyhood. Almost all the stories about his early life have come from others. A few are considered to be legends. The events told here are thought to be true.

Nearly everyone lived on farms in colonial America. The Fulton farm stood along the Conowingo Creek in a township called Little Britain. Their two-story farmhouse was surrounded by almost 400 acres of land. Robert lived here until he was six years old. His father, Robert Fulton, Sr., did not succeed as a farmer. Unable to repay his loans, he sold the farm and almost everything they owned.

The family moved to Lancaster, about 30 miles to the north of the farm. Robert was eight years old when his father died in 1774. At this time, his mother, Mary Smith Fulton, sent him to a school run by a teacher named Caleb Johnson.

In 1775, the colonists' struggle against the British turned into an armed fight. On July 4, 1776, the Declaration of Independence was signed, proclaiming the colonies free from British rule. Lancaster became a supply center of guns, clothing, food, wagons, and horses for the Continental Army. Robert is said to have learned several skills from the local tradespeople.

Robert was 15 when the British General Charles Cornwallis surrendered to American General George Washington in 1781.

Robert Fulton

About this time, Robert traveled to Philadelphia to earn income for himself and the family. He went to work as an apprentice to a jeweler, a position requiring steady hands and artistic skill for creating fine intricate designs.

Although the first census of Philadelphia gave the population as just 28,522, there were only a handful of other small cities in the United States. Philadelphia was a good place for Fulton to begin his career. Some of the greatest statesmen, business leaders, inventors, and artisans of America lived there. It was a city where a boy's ambitions could grow.

By the time he was 17, Fulton was also working as a painter of miniature portraits. His artistic skill increased along with his reputation as a gentleman. His social skills helped him impress the influential people of his time. He set up his own shop when he was 20. About this time, Fulton also became acquainted with Benjamin Franklin, a famous statesman and one of the most respected of American inventors and scientists of the time.

In 1786, Fulton visited a warm springs in Virginia to treat a lung illness. Several wealthy and influential people also came to the springs for their health. Some of them were impressed with Fulton. They suggested that he study in Europe to advance his career as an artist. Fulton took their encouragement seriously. After his health improved, he returned home with a European excursion in mind.

He saved some money, bought his mother a farm, and then set sail for England to meet the famous artist Benjamin West. He carried a letter of introduction with him, said to have been written by Franklin. Over time, Fulton would meet many interesting men and women, several of whom would have a strong influence on his life.

Benjamin West seemed an ideal choice as an artistic mentor. He came from circumstances very similar to Fulton's. He had also lived in Lancaster and was born on a farm in the county next to Fulton's. Twenty-seven years older than Fulton, West was considered by many to be one of the top living artists. He was the official history painter for King George III and an esteemed member of the Royal Academy. Fulton arrived at Benjamin West's London residence in 1787. He was impressed with West and aspired to follow in his footsteps.

West recommended a house on Charlotte Street where Fulton could stay. The lodgings included a workroom, bedroom, food, and other comforts for one guinea a week. Fulton had brought only 40 guineas with him from America. A guinea was a gold coin worth 252 pennies, or pence, in England.

Fulton soon found there were a great number of aspiring and talented artists in England. London was a city of over 700,000 people, much larger than Philadelphia. He earned a few commissions for painting portraits but otherwise lived on loans and charity. He said, however, that he was never "in absolute want— heaven has been kind to me and I am thankful."

After trying to succeed as an artist for seven years, Fulton found he was still far from receiving the recognition that came to Benjamin West or English artists such as Thomas Gainsborough and Sir Joshua Reynolds or even other Americans such as John Singleton Copley and Gilbert Stuart. He wondered if there might be some other area in which he might achieve greatness.

At the age of 28, Fulton changed careers. His drawing and other creative talents were useful in the emerging field of engineering. As he improved his engineering skills, he began to find ways to improve inventions. These efforts eventually led to the creations for which he is best remembered.

His first interest was the English craft work being done with marble. Seeing a way to improve on their cutting methods, he invented a marble-cutting machine. His invention was so well liked, that it was awarded a silver medal by the Society for the Encouragement of Arts, Commerce, and Manufactures in 1794.

This success came soon in comparison to the several years he had spent painting. He looked around England for other fields of endeavor that might benefit from new inventions. He chose canal construction as his next concern. Some canals being built in England were very profitable and they were considered the modern way to transport goods across the country.

Lord Stanhope led a committee entrusted to build a new canal. Fulton read the committee's land survey report and thought he saw a better way to build the canal. He wrote to Lord Stanhope with his suggestions. Lord Stanhope answered and soon became a significant figure in Fulton's new career. Lord Stanhope was an inventor, too. His inventions included a special lever, a calculator, a thermometer, and others. In his letters to Fulton, he stressed the importance of tests to prove the efficiency of inventions.

Stanhope was also involved in building an early steamboat. Fulton expressed his interest in this, as well. They wrote to each other about ideas for inventions. Fulton tested steamboat models occasionally over the next several years. At this time, however, Fulton chose to concentrate on canal innovations.

Canals were a safer proposition; their usefulness was already accepted by the public. Steam-powered boats were still curious contraptions. Few people would risk their lives or their money on them. Fulton wanted to invest his time and efforts profitably.

One of his earliest inventions was designed for transporting boats between canal courses on uneven land. Boats could be floated on either of two giant wheeled carriages or tubs. Riding on iron or wood rails, these tubs would be raised or lowered on stone ramps to the next level of the canal. Controlled by rope pulleys, one carriage served as the counter-weight to the second.

A second creation was a canal-digging invention. The machine had four wheels and was pulled by horses. The turning of the rear wheels rotated a series of gears that operated an earth scoop and a propeller that knocked the dirt to the side of the canal.

For all of his drawings and plans, the Peak Forest Company gave Fulton a hundred guineas and paid for the printing of 200 copies of his first book. Fulton called his book *Treatise on the Improvement of Canal Navigation*. It was published on March 1, 1796. Giving official notice of his new career, he authored the book as R. Fulton, civil engineer.

Fulton tried to encourage others to support his canal construction concepts. His ideas gained little support in England. Then, in 1797, John Church expressed interest in building canals in America. Church was an investor about to return there soon. He paid Fulton for a one-fourth share in his canal venture. Fulton said he would try to arrive in America by June 1798, after he patented his canal inventions in France.

Fulton arrived in the Republic of France in the summer of 1797. The time seemed right. England and France were trying to negotiate a truce to their long-standing rivalry. The French Revolution was also calming down. Fulton liked the ideal of the free republics that France and America represented. He also thought he would earn a better income in lands free of rule by lords and kings.

Soon during his stay, Fulton became close friends of the American diplomat and commodities speculator Joel Barlow. He and his wife Ruth invited Fulton to live with them in Paris. He gladly accepted their invitation and was treated like a son by the Barlows.

Fulton submitted his application for a patent on his canal invention and waited for approval. During this time he also wrote some manuscripts about free trade, the unhindered shipment of goods across the world. One of the obstacles to Fulton's ideal of free trade was the British navy. England had the largest and most powerful naval fleet on earth. The navy sank the ships and blockaded the ports of several countries, including America and France. An invention that could stop this tyranny would be welcomed—perhaps an invisible ship that could emerge from the sea and strike without warning. It is likely at this time that Fulton learned of the inventions of David Bushnell.

Bushnell was the first American submarine inventor. He invented a one-person, seven-foot submarine that floated like a turtle sticking its head out of the water. He also invented the first torpedo, a container filled with gunpowder set to explode next to the hull of a ship. His submarine was used against British ships during the American Revolution. It was not successful, however. He had trouble getting further support and gave up on his invention after a few years.

Fulton thought he could engineer the best submarine. In December 1797, he sent his first submarine proposal to the leaders of France.

"Considering the great importance of diminishing the power of the British Fleets," Fulton wrote, "I have contemplated the construction of a mechanical *nautilus* . . . Citizens hoping that this engine will tend to give liberty to the seas; it is of importance that the experiment should be proved as soon as possible."

In February 1798, he learned that his proposal for creating a submarine had not been accepted. This outcome was not surprising since he had not submitted a model or description of his submarine. His disappointment was compensated by the joy of finding that his canal invention patent had been approved.

With this approval, Fulton should have been preparing to return to America as he had planned with John Church. Fulton still wanted to see if his canal ideas would be used in France, however, and he still had high hopes for his submarine. Thinking that he would remain just a little longer, he ended up staying in France for six more years.

In the summer of 1798, Fulton informed the French Marine Ministry that he had now built a "beautiful model of the *Nautilus* five feet long complete in all its parts." A commission came to see Fulton on August 7. They were impressed with his show. They recommended that Fulton be paid for his work and for his future experiments. The French leaders were informed, but they did not approve the request.

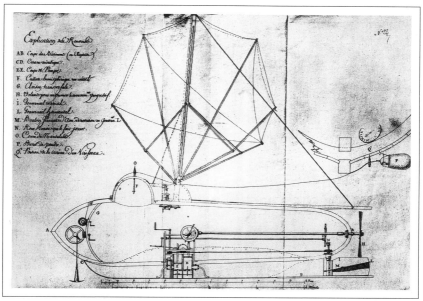

Fulton's first sketch of the Nautilus, from his 1798 report in France.
AB. Body of Boat (Ellipsoid); CD. Metal keel; EE. Pump cylinders; F.
Conning tower (hemisphere of metal); G. Cross bulkhead; H. Propeller; I.
Vertical rudder; L. Horizontal Rudder; M. Fulcrum for Horizontal Rudder; N.
Gears for Rudder Operation; O. Horn (Spike) of the Nautilus;
P. Torpedo [on cable]; Q. The bottom of a boat.
(National Museum of American History,
Smithsonian Institution, Negative no. 43245)

Fulton continued to concentrate on his canal and submarine ventures. In 1799, Fulton wrote his mother, "Still Europe holds me, not by ties of affection but by the bonds of business with which I am ever so much engaged that I have not had time even to fall in love . . . it is my intention," he added, "to reserve all my affections for some amicable American whose customs and manners I prefer."

The French leadership was suddenly overthrown on November 9, 1799. In December 1799, a new constitution and consulate were formed and approved by the French lawmakers. The new leader of France was First Consul Napoleon Bonaparte.

Fulton would now have to impress Napoleon to get government approval for his canals and submarines. He thought he had "every reason to hope from Bonaparte the welcome, the encouragement that have been so long refused by the Directors and Ministers."

Without waiting further for government financing, Fulton decided to build his submarine. In April 1800, he informed Napoleon's newly appointed marine minister that the submarine was almost completed.

On June 13, 1800, Fulton stood on the bank of the Seine River in Paris. He was there to give a show of his completed submarine. The trim, six-foot-tall Fulton and his assistant entered the newly completed *Nautilus* and closed the hatch. The crowd watched as the submarine slowly traveled across the river. Then it vanished beneath the water. Twenty minutes passed. Some distance away, the *Nautilus* slowly emerged. Then it sank again and re-emerged at the starting location. The mast was raised and they triumphantly sailed across the river to the sound of cheers. The show was a success.

The submarine shell was three times longer than Bushnell's and could carry a crew of four. Along with other innovations, Fulton's submarine was the first to use one type of propulsion for the surface and another for submerged travel, the first to use stern (tail) diving planes (or "wings" as he called them), and the first to use a compressed air supply.

Fulton tried tests in several other French ports. He soon added a deck to the *Nautilus* so that it would look like an ordinary boat on the surface. He even sailed the submarine for 70 miles along the coast of France.

In September 1800, he and his crew tried to attack two English ships during a storm. The English learned of Fulton's plans, however, and quickly sailed away.

With winter approaching, Fulton put the *Nautilus* in storage. When he returned in the spring, he found that the bolts of the *Nautilus* were rusted and that the submarine was not seaworthy.

After getting favorable reports from some eminent scientists and his marine minister, Napoleon approved some funds to get the *Nautilus* in working order and to build torpedoes.

Fulton tested the refitted submarine in Brest. It was here that he used his compressed air tank for the first time. The *Nautilus* performed well but was still leaky. Fulton said he wished to make a larger, stronger submarine that could carry six people and be able to submerge to 80 feet below the surface.

Fulton was shortly notified that Napoleon wanted to see the *Nautilus*. Considering the leaking submarine no longer useful, Fulton had already taken it apart and sold the pieces. Funding for a new submarine was not approved.

Fulton continued to seek support for a new submarine. In the meantime, he found another project to fill his time.

In December 1801, the U.S. diplomat Robert R. Livingston and his wife arrived in France. Livingston enjoyed an interesting career. Having been a member of the Continental Congress, a member of the Declaration of Independence committee, a chancellor of New York, and George Washington's secretary of foreign affairs, he also owned vast amounts of land and held two U.S. invention patents.

Livingston was also a financier of steamboats. He tried to have a steamboat built in America. After much time and expense, he slowly came to the conclusion that he did not know how to build a successful steamboat.

Fortunately, he became acquainted with Fulton in 1802. Livingston saw the engineer and inventor he needed in Fulton. Fulton saw the financial and political supporter he needed in Robert Livingston. They agreed to build a steamboat together.

Fulton completed a steamboat model in May and then tested various changes. In 1803, he built a 70-foot version. He suffered a setback when the boat sank in a storm. Working 24 hours straight without eating or resting, he led a crew that recovered the remains. The steamboat was soon rebuilt, tested on the Seine River, and called a "brilliant invention" by the French press.

Over this time, Fulton carefully applied his invention and engineering skills. As an inventor, he studied all the ways of propelling a steamboat and experimented with various paddle types and arrangements. As an engineer, he performed calculations of ship and engine sizes, shapes, weights, water resistance, and loading capacities.

After an extended stay in England, Fulton gained the approval for the export of a custom engine from the British steam engine makers Matthew Boulton and James Watt. The engine was waiting for him when he arrived in America in 1806.

By 1807, Fulton had his new steamboat built and ready for use. It was 150 feet long and had a large paddle wheel on each side. He first called it simply, *The Steamboat*. Skeptical onlookers called it "Fulton's Folly." Fulton heard their comments. "While we were passing off from the wharf, which was crowded with spectators," he wrote, "I heard a number of sarcastic remarks. This is the way in which ignorant men compliment what they call philosophers and projectors."

His friend Livingston had greater confidence. He invited all his friends and relatives to come on the first voyage. Told by Livingston that it would be something to remember all their lives, they came dressed in fine clothes for the gala event.

About a dozen women were present among the 40 passengers. Harriet Livingston, a young cousin of Robert Livingston, was one of them. She had recently become the "amicable American" who attracted the affection of Fulton.

The launching of the steamboat on the Hudson River occurred at one o'clock on the summer afternoon of August 17, 1807. Fulton wrote, "All were still incredulous . . . We left the fair city of New York; [and] passed through the romantic and ever-varying scenery."

In a country used to vessels guided by sails or oars, *The Steamboat* was an odd sight. Its large steam engine machinery and two paddle-wheels were without coverings. Some said it looked like a floating sawmill set on fire. With the side-wheels splashing,

The North River of Clermont *churning on the Hudson River between Albany and New York City in the early 1800s.*
(National Museum of American History,
Smithsonian Institution,
Negative no. 37977)

wooden deck creaking, and engine belching, the steamboat easily gained the attention of everyone along the way.

The Steamboat covered 110 miles on the first day and arrived in Clermont, the home of Robert Livingston. A celebration was held, and according to a second Livingston cousin, Helen, the engagement of Robert Fulton and Harriet Livingston was announced.

The steamboat continued on to Albany the following day. After the return trip to New York, a regular service between the two cities was started. Soon rebuilt and widened, *The Steamboat* was called *The North River* and also *The North River of Clermont*. Within a few years, writers were calling the famous steamboat simply, the *Clermont*.

By whatever name, the steamboat was a success. On January 7, 1808, Harriet and Robert were married. They eventually had four children.

Over the following years, Fulton built several steamboats, constantly improving their design, comfort, and speed. He wrote to his first mentor, Benjamin West,

> *I am endeavoring to be in the mechanic arts what you are in the fine art of painting by steady attention to one of the most useful kind, I mean steamboats . . . in a few more years we shall have the most elegant, cheap, rapid and extensive inland communications in the world.*

Fulton's enthusiastic prediction proved to be correct. Although he died on February 23, 1815, after complications from an icy winter chill, his competitors carried on the steamboat construction tradition. Through steady competition, steamboats became so elegant they were called "floating palaces." Their speed and convenience created the country's best transportation system.

As the first commercially successful engine-powered transportation, Fulton's steamboat led the way for other engine-powered inventions. Engine-powered boats were soon followed by locomotives and steamships, then automobiles and aircraft.

One of Robert Fulton's strengths was his certainty that he had greatness in him. His first attempts failed to bring acclaim, yet he tried all his life to demonstrate his greatness. He finally succeeded by trying to outdo all others in engineering talent and preciseness in the design and construction of a steamboat. He knew he was not the first inventor in this area, but he tried to be the best.

Earlier steamboats had been invented by several others before Fulton, such as the Marquis de Jouffroy in 1783, John Fitch and James Rumsey in 1787, and William Symington in 1788. Due to customer, design, or financial problems, however, there were no steamboats in business by 1805. A continuous, successful steamboat industry started with Fulton in 1807. Fulton learned to make his steamboats large, comfortable, and reliable to attract sufficient customers. Using his engineering skills, he designed his inventions for efficiency according to calculations and thought, not simply trial and error. Fulton was also able to turn a tinkerer's dream into a commercial success by acquiring a loyal partner who had the financial skills and customer contacts that he lacked.

As well as being an inventor, engineer, and artist, Robert Fulton was also a visionary. He was a doer *and* a dreamer. Although his inventions are inspiring, his ideas on free trade, "the freedom of the seas," and efficient international communication are inspiring to many, as well. As one of his early biographers, Henry Winram Dickinson, wrote,

> *As a thinker he saw clearly that free trade intercourse between nations, universal disarmament, the spread of education and of political liberty among all people, were necessary to the progress of the human race. But he saw more than this, for having imagination and a wide outlook he realized the needs of advancing civilization and set himself with pluck and perseverance to supply them.*

Chronology

November 14, 1765	Robert Fulton is born in Little Britain Township in Pennsylvania
1794	changes career from art to engineering; is awarded silver medal for marble-cutting invention
1796	publishes *Treatise on the Improvement of Canal Navigation*
1800	starts *Nautilus* submarine tests in the ocean along the coast of France
1807	launches *The Steamboat* on Hudson River in New York
February 23, 1815	Fulton dies in New York City

Further Reading

Flexner, James Thomas. *Steamboats Come True: American Inventors in Action*. Boston: Little, Brown and Company, 1944, 1978. Good overview of steamboat inventors, well researched.

Hill, Ralph Nading. *Robert Fulton and the Steamboat*. New York: Random House, 1954. Entertaining. Although it contains legends and some fictional conversation, this book contains more facts than most Fulton biographies for young adults.

Parsons, William Barclay. *Robert Fulton and the Submarine*. New York: AMS Press, Inc., 1967 [1922]. Good reference material on Fulton's submarine efforts.

Philip, Cynthia Owen. *Robert Fulton: A Biography*. New York: Franklin Watts, 1985. Very thorough biography, well researched. Written for adult readers.

Samuel F. B. Morse
(1791–1872)

*Samuel F. B. Morse. An engraving by John Sartain
from a photograph by Mathew Brady.*
(National Portrait Gallery, Smithsonian Institution
NPG.86.39)

*I*n the Cove of Cork on the coast of Ireland, Samuel Morse tested a special telegraph cable in 1857. Almost as soon as he tapped the telegraph key, a clear sound chimed at the other end.

Stowed on two steamships, the coiled cable (about 2,500 miles long) was scheduled to be laid across the ocean floor to Canada. After 12 months of effort, the two continents were finally connected. The cable was also tied to telegraph lines leading to the United States, Continental Europe, and Asia.

Queen Victoria of England and President James Buchanan of the United States sent the first official transatlantic greetings on August 16, 1858. Soon, hundreds of telegrams were sent.

Morse's success had a profound effect on inter-continental communications. Before, sailing ships had been the fastest means of communication between Europe and America. With wind and weather changes, the trip took from one to four months. Then, steamships shortened this time to two weeks. The telegraph shortened it to a split *second*. The telegraphs used on the transatlantic cable and on almost all the lines in the world were based on the invention of Samuel Morse. His creation was the first to put electricity to commercial use.

Samuel Finley Breese Morse was born in a rented house in Charlestown, Massachusetts, on April 27, 1791. The two-story house stood at the foot of Breed's Hill, the site of a June 1775 conflict in the American Revolution.

Finley, as Morse was called as a boy, was the eldest child. When he was almost three, his brother Sidney was born. His youngest brother Richard arrived two years later. Of 11 children born to Jedidiah and Elizabeth Ann Morse, they were the only ones to survive infancy.

At four years of age, Finley was sent to the school of "Old Ma'am Rand." Too weak and old to leave her chair, Rand used a cane to control the little classroom. One time, Finley used a pin to scratch her portrait on a chest of drawers. His teacher pinned him to her dress. As he struggled to get free, she rewarded his efforts with a whack to his shoulders.

Finley could not stand still for very long. He often skipped from one activity to another. Finley's father likened him to the Hare in the children's fable, and to steady and stubborn Sidney the Tortoise.

Finley was sent to a preparatory school about 20 miles away from his home when he was seven. He studied his school subjects hastily. His marks were sometimes high and sometimes low. He received eight demerits in spelling and 18 for whispering in class.

His father and mother tried to encourage Finley by offering him rewards of cakes, pies, and books for good grades. His father, who was a minister, advised Finley to attend to one thing at a time and try to do his best. He also asked him to keep a daily journal, give an accounting of his expenses, and write a letter every Sunday on the church sermons he attended.

Finley improved enough scholastically to be accepted at Yale College, which he entered in 1805. (At that time, taking entrance exams as a young teenager was not uncommon for college-minded students.) Of all his courses, two subjects excited him the most: chemistry and electricity. "I am very much pleased with chemistry," he wrote in a letter home to his parents, "There are many very beautiful and surprising experiments performed, which are likewise very useful." His teacher, Professor Benjamin Silliman, included lectures on electrical batteries like the one invented by Alessandro Volta in 1800. Silliman would take them apart and show the students how they worked.

Finley especially enjoyed his classes in electricity taught by Professor Jeremiah Day. One of the experiments that Professor Day performed involved sending electrical current through a series of metal pieces held close to each other in a loop. In the dark, the current could be seen flashing around the circuit. In a second experiment, folds of paper were placed near the tight spacings between the metal conductors. As the electricity sparked across the short gaps, it left marks in the paper.

To make the electricity lessons memorable, the students were invited to form a circle and hold hands. With the addition of current to their circle, they all received a light electric surprise at the same moment. "I never received an electric shock before," wrote Finley, "It felt as if some person had struck me a slight blow across the arms."

Years later, Morse wrote,

The fact that the presence of electricity can be made visible in any desired part of the circuit was the crude seed which took root in my mind, and grew up into form, and ripened into the invention of the Telegraph.

In his spare time, Morse indulged his childhood urges and covered the walls of his school dormitory room with sketches and paintings. He often invited fellow students to visit. He drew sketches of them scrambling on their hands and knees up a steep hill. He called the sketch *Freshman Climbing the Hill of Science*. One student asked Morse if he would paint his likeness. The impressive result attracted similar requests from several other students and teachers.

Morse enjoyed this attention. At 18, he started to earn income at the school as a painter of miniature portraits. Robert Fulton had started the same career at almost the same age, although he belonged to an earlier generation. By this time, 1809, Fulton was 44 and busy with his steamboats.

As his college graduation grew near, Morse had great plans for the future. Like Robert Fulton before him, he wanted to visit Europe to improve his painting skills. Europe offered more advantages for talented artists than America did. Learning that the American painter Washington Allston had just returned from Europe and was visiting in Boston, next to Morse's hometown of Charlestown, Morse wrote to his father and mother, stating his intention to study with Allston during the coming winter. Then in the spring, Morse hoped to go along with him to England.

Morse's father replied, "On the subject of your future pursuits we will converse when I see you." He did not agree to his son's plans. Instead, he got him a job as a book clerk in Boston.

Trying to handle two careers, Morse worked at the bookshop during the day and painted in the evening. He often visited Allston's studio and received guidance and encouragement. He tried his best to create fine paintings. Allston and Gilbert Stuart, another well-known painter, appreciated Morse's efforts. They were able to convince Morse's father of his son's talent, and Jedidiah reconsidered and agreed to let Morse go to England with Allston. Finley was overjoyed.

Morse and Allston landed on the English coast in August 1811. After a week's journey by horse-pulled carriage, they arrived in London. Samuel, as Morse then liked to be called, wrote his first letter home. He said, "While I am writing I can imagine mother wishing that she could hear of my arrival, and thinking of thousands of accidents which may have befallen me. I wish that in an instant I could communicate the information: but three thousand miles are not passed over in an instant, and we must wait four long weeks before we can hear from each other."

The day after Morse sent this letter, Allston introduced him to the artist Benjamin West. At 74, West was still extending hospitality to aspiring artists. Allston had been his student 10 years earlier. West continued to paint large historical paintings and was now the head of England's Royal Academy of Arts. Like Robert Fulton, Morse was extremely impressed with him.

Morse enjoyed relating an early episode in his studies with West. Having completed a drawing of a figure with great care, he brought it to West. West studied the work and commended him. Morse was honored by the master's praise. Then West suggested that Morse finish the drawing, catching him by surprise. He thought it was completed. West then calmly pointed out some sections to improve. Morse worked to correct his drawing for a full week. When he was satisfied, he showed the drawing to West again. West was full of flattery for Morse's efforts, but once more suggested that Morse complete the task.

After returning to his workroom, Morse spent several days refining every line and curve. Then he visited West again, hoping to hear the end of West's suggestions about finishing the work.

Samuel F. B. Morse self-portrait in 1812.
(National Portrait Gallery, Smithsonian Institution
NPG.80.208)

18

West was almost overwhelmed by the beauty of Samuel's drawing. He said it was exceedingly good. Again, however, he suggested that Morse try to find areas that could be improved.

Morse sighed. He thought it was complete *this* time.

West saw that Morse had tried his best. He agreed that he could not find sections still left to improve either. He said Morse had learned more by this drawing than he would have accomplished in twice the time by a dozen half-finished ones. It is not numerous drawings, West said, but the *character of one*, which makes an artist. *Finish* one picture, and you are a painter, he stressed.

Morse was learning to concentrate and complete his work in the best way. West's advice for a painter would serve equally well for an inventor. *Finish* one *invention* and you are an *inventor*.

Morse enjoyed greater artistic success in England than Robert Fulton had. In 1813 he won a gold medal for a sculpture of Hercules and his entry ranked in the top dozen paintings at the exhibition of the Royal Academy of Arts. By 1815, Morse felt he could say, "My ambition is to be enlisted in the constellation of genius now rising in this country; I wish . . . to strive to shine the brightest."

That October, Morse returned to America. Shortly thereafter, he became attracted to 17-year-old Lucretia Walker of Concord, New Hampshire. Soon they were writing love letters to each other and before the end of the year, their engagement was announced.

Except for some sidetracks, Morse tried to earn a living as an artist for the following 30 years. He painted over 250 portraits. Among his subjects were James Monroe, the president of the United States; Eli Whitney, inventor of the cotton gin; and Noah Webster, of dictionary fame. Morse also painted *The Hall of Representatives* and the *Gallery of the Louvre*.

Samuel and Lucretia married in 1818, and they had five children by 1825, although only three survived infancy. Morse hoped to obtain a house for his family with earnings from his historical paintings, but there was almost no interest in this kind of art. People wanted only portraits of themselves or their loved ones. Leaving his family in the care of relatives, Morse searched for new patrons in several states.

The greatness that Morse sought seemed to elude him. "I have been told several times," he wrote, "that I was born one hundred years too soon for the arts in our country."

His luck seemed to improve in 1825, when he was awarded a substantial commission to paint the French officer the Marquis de Lafayette who was visiting America. Morse gave his family the good news and then went to Washington to paint Lafayette's portrait.

Lucretia seemed in good health when he left. While Samuel was away, however, she became very ill with a heart complication. Morse's father wrote to tell him of his wife's condition. Samuel did not receive the letter in time. Lucretia died before he was even aware that she was sick. Morse was deeply shocked. He did not receive the letter announcing his wife's death until four days after the fact. In the meantime, he had written letters to her assuming she was still alive. His wish for instant communication, especially with loved ones, still needed to be fulfilled.

Seven years later, in 1832, Samuel saw the solution. He was on a sailing vessel, *The Sully*, returning to America after a three-year painting tour in Europe. Some of the passengers talked about the wonders of electricity.

Morse was still interested in this subject. Five years earlier, he had attended lectures about the new discoveries in electricity and electromagnetism. An electromagnet invented by William Sturgeon of England was demonstrated. When electricity was sent through wire coiled around an iron bar, the bar attracted other metal containing iron. In the years after the lectures, the instructor had visited Morse several times to share his enthusiasm for electricity.

One fellow passenger aboard the *Sully* asked if electricity was slowed in traveling through long wire lengths. Another who had studied Benjamin Franklin's experiments on the subject said no. A spark appeared at the same time using short or long wires.

Then the idea essential to the conception of an electric telegraph took hold in Morse's mind. "If the presence of electricity can be made visible in any part of the circuit," he wrote, "I see no reason why intelligence may not be transmitted instantaneously by electricity."

Morse was so excited by this idea he could barely sleep that night. He filled his journal with the *complete* plans for a working telegraph and code. Morse drew an electromagnet that would close a lever on contact and open when contact was released. He even imagined a clock-driven recording device that would run a strip of paper under the lever. A pencil would be attached to the lever. When a short contact was made, a short line would be recorded. With a long contact, a longer line would appear.

Independently, he thought of what eventually evolved into Morse Code. Morse set up a series of dots and dashes to represent numbers to be combined to form words. Letters were later added to the code so that a numbered dictionary would not be necessary. Morse also envisioned having his electrical wires enclosed in tubes to be buried underground.

Almost as soon as Morse set foot on American ground, he rushed to start on his telegraph. Unfortunately, he soon ran out of money and had to look for other work to support himself and his three children. Morse became a professor of sculpture and painting at the recently founded University of the City of New York. At first, he received no funds except for fees from his students.

Morse's first telegraph, made by hand out of wood and metal scraps in 1837. The device in the lower front is the sender and the larger device behind is the receiver.
(Division of Electricity and Modern Physics, National Museum of American History, Smithsonian Institution, Negative no. 14,593-B)

Nineteenth-Century Inventors

Living as cheaply as he could and using simple materials, Morse spent long lonely hours on his invention. He was charged a low annual fee for the use of some rooms at the university where he set up his telegraph. While his relatives took care of his children at their homes, Samuel taught, ate, and slept in one of the classrooms.

On his own, out of wood and metal scraps, Morse built his telegraph sender, set up his batteries and wire, and received messages on his telegraph recorder. Then he invited fellow professors and other friends to see it work.

The first sender had a long wooden arm that was raised and lowered by the notches on metal clips that were shaped according to the early Morse Code. The simpler design of a short metal sending key and a metal "sounder" telegraph receiving instrument were developed over time.

Morse was probably lucky that he completed his invention before exposing it to the public. By continuing on his own, Morse became a telegraph expert with firsthand knowledge. He thought he was the first in his field. He might never have tried to build a telegraph if he had been fully informed about the current knowledge of electrical experiments.

Andre-Marie Ampère, Joseph Henry, and others had suggested the idea of electric telegraphs before Morse. Leonard Gale, a science professor at the same university as Morse, informed Morse of the work of Joseph Henry. Henry conducted experiments with electromagnets and learned to increase their strength by increasing the number of wire wraps around the iron bar.

Gale also told Morse that he thought the telegraph would not work beyond 20 miles. The experiments of others had shown that a current weakened as it traveled through wire.

Morse already had a working telegraph invention. He wasn't going to be stopped now. He explained to Gale his idea of an electrical relay. An electromagnet with its own battery supply could be connected to the wires every 20 miles or so. When this electromagnet closed, a fresh current would be sent along the next 20 miles. In this way, a message could be sent around the world.

Later, Morse learned that the current could be strengthened by simply adding more battery cells. The law discovered by Georg Simon Ohm in 1826 stated that electrical current is equal to voltage (electrical force) divided by resistance (the opposition to the force). Increasing the voltage with more cells (containers) of electricity-producing chemicals increased the current.

Samuel F. B. Morse

Although Henry did not reveal some of his work for several years, he also experimented with relays, worked on how to increase current with battery cells, and devised a simple electric bell that could have been used as a telegraph instrument. However, Henry was trying to make scientific discoveries, not inventions. He never patented his work and, in 1842, he said in a letter that he preferred the telegraph invented by Samuel Morse.

Gale was convinced that Morse's invention was the best, too. He bought a share in Morse's telegraph enterprise. Then a student, Alfred Vail, visited Morse's studio in 1837. Morse's explanation for long distance telegraphy convinced him, too. He became Morse's second partner. Morse gave credit to Vail for the telegraph's eventual success. "Fulton had a Livingston to aid him . . . I had Vail." Vail said, "I feel, Professor Morse, that if I am worth anything it will be wholly attributable to your kindness."

In 1838, the partners exhibited the telegraph to Congress. As Fulton did with his submarine, they sought government financial support instead of private financing. Like Fulton, they encountered similar failure; their proposal was not accepted.

With little knowledge of finance, Morse continued to seek government assistance. Five years later, he approached the Congress again. "My means to defray my expenses . . . are nearly all gone, and if, by any means, the bill should fail in the Senate, I shall return to New York with the fraction of a dollar in my pocket."

Fortunately, this time his bill passed, but just barely. Although some of the supporters did not trust the telegraph, they trusted Samuel Morse. One senator, however, admitted to scanning Morse's face for signs of insanity. Annie Ellsworth, the patent commissioner's daughter, brought Morse the good news. In gratitude, Morse granted her the honor of choosing the first telegraph message.

The first official intercity telegraph line connected Washington to Baltimore. Due to difficulties with underground installation, the line was strung on poles. On May 24, 1844, it was ready for use.

In the Supreme Court chamber of the Capitol Building, Annie Ellsworth showed Morse the words she had selected for the occasion. As he tapped the telegraph key, the code for "What hath God wrought!" flashed like lightning to the other end of the circuit.

The success of Morse's telegraph soon became known across the country. By 1851, over 50 telegraph companies started stretching wires. Ten years later, telegraph lines laced the country from the Atlantic to the Pacific, even before the completion of the transcontinental railroad. In five more years, almost half a million miles of lines in America, Europe, and Asia would be connected.

The new occupation of telegrapher was created. Teenagers often came to fill these openings. One of the thousands of these young telegraphers was a fellow called Thomas Alva Edison.

Time and space seemed shorter now. Perhaps of most importance to Morse, loved ones could now have access to instant communication. The telegraph became as important to people as the postal service. When time was of the essence, the telegraph was the first choice for important business and personal communication.

Morse soon left the business end of the telegraph enterprise in the hands of others. However, he was called to contest lawsuits filed by his competitors. Although a few European inventors tried telegraphs that silently moved magnetic needles, the Morse telegraph soon became the world standard. Morse received medals and honors from several countries grateful for his invention.

He eventually retired in comfort in his own custom-built home overlooking the Hudson River. He even bought a second house in New York City on 22nd Street. Like Cyrus Hall McCormick, Morse enjoyed giving money to his favorite churches and colleges.

On June 10, 1871, Morse was honored with the unveiling of his statue in Central Park in New York City. Cyrus Hall McCormick was among the important guests at the occasion. Morse attended a special ceremony that evening at the Academy of Music on 14th Street. Cyrus Field, the backer of the transatlantic cable; Horace Greeley, a well-known publisher and editor; and William Orton, the president of the Western Union Company, the largest telegraph enterprise in the country, were present. Annie Ellsworth was there, too. Orton informed the audience that the telegraph instrument in front of them was connected on open lines to every city in the United States and Canada. The telegraph sent Morse's message. "Greetings and thanks to the telegraph community throughout the world. Glory to God in the highest, on earth peace, goodwill to men." Morse then tapped the letters: "S. F. B. Morse." The audience rose to their feet and cheered.

"Thus the Father of the telegraph bids farewell to his children," said Orton. On April 2, 1872, Morse died at his home. In his lifetime, the telegraph was the top instrument for long-distance communications. The telephone would not be invented for another four years.

Morse's first official biographer, Samuel I. Prime, who knew Morse in his later life, wrote, "He had faith in God and strong confidence in his own ability to make the instrument practically successful . . . He studied the strictest economy . . . [and] engaged in a work which to all others seemed *visionary*."

Congressman James Blaine, the speaker of the House of Representatives at the time, summed up Morse's career:

Less than thirty years ago, a man of genius and learning was an earnest petitioner before Congress for a small pecuniary [monetary] aid . . . The little thread of wire placed as a timid experiment between the national capital and a neighboring city, grew and lengthened, and multiplied with almost the rapidity of the electric current that darted along its iron nerves, until, within his own lifetime, continent was bound unto continent, hemisphere answered through the ocean's depths unto hemisphere, and an encircled globe flashed forth . . . in the unmatched elements of a grand achievement.

Chronology

April 27, 1791	Samuel F. B. Morse is born in Charlestown, Massachusetts
1805	enters Yale College; takes classes in electricity and chemistry
1809	earns income as a portrait painter
1811	arrives in England to study art under Benjamin West
1815	returns to America after winning sculpture award
1832	conceives his telegraph invention
1844	connects first intercity line between Washington and Baltimore; sends "What hath God wrought!"
1857	tests first transatlantic telegraph cable
April 2, 1872	dies in New York City

Further Reading

Math, Irwin. *Morse, Marconi, and You.* New York: Charles Scribner's Sons, 1979. With drawings and text, this book shows how to build the Morse telegraph, Bell telephone, and Edison carbon transmitter from common materials. Contains interesting electrical experiments and projects. Written for young adults.

Tiner, John Hudson. *Samuel F. B. Morse: Artist With A Message.* Milford, Michigan: Mott Media, 1987. Although it contains conjectured dialogue, this book is one of the better Morse biographies for young adults.

Charles Goodyear
(1800–1860)

*Charles Goodyear. Painted by G. P. A. Healy in
Paris in 1855.*
(Goodyear Tire and Rubber Co.)

*T*he year 1855 began as one of the best years of Charles
Goodyear's life. Continuing his European tour, Goodyear was in
France to exhibit his invention at the world's fair in Paris. Built to
surpass the site of his first international showing, the English
Crystal Palace exhibitions of 1851, France's Exposition Universelle would be the setting for Goodyear's greatest showcase.

Like many American inventors, Goodyear thought his success
incomplete without the recognition of Europe. He spent $50,000,

an extravagant amount in those times, on two elegant exhibition courts.

These courts were filled with items based on Goodyear's creation—vulcanized rubber. This substance was unlike anything the world had ever known. Fine furniture, jewelry, portraits, and fashionable articles of clothing, all using the new rubber, were on display for the international spectators to admire.

Goodyear was awarded the exposition's Grand Medal. To top even this honor, Emperor Napoleon III awarded him the Cross of the Legion of Honor. On one occasion that summer, Charles even rode with the emperor in his carriage! Goodyear's joy was to be short-lived, however.

Before the end of the year, Goodyear was locked up in a cell at Clichy prison in Paris for a few weeks. Goodyear had spent far more on the exhibition than he could afford, and imprisonment was a common fate for people who did not pay their bills.

This low moment was a typical one in Goodyear's life. He never learned basic business skills, to the detriment of his and his family's future. He had one quality that was exceptional, however, and that was his extraordinary confidence in his invention.

Charles was born to Amasa and Cynthia Goodyear on December 29, 1800, in New Haven, Connecticut, near the site of Yale College. His parents later had five other children. They were Henry, Robert, Harriet, Nelson, and Amasa, Jr.

Charles's father was a trader of goods and a manufacturer of buttons, spoons, and scythes. He also took care of a farm. Due to all his farming and business chores, young Charles had limited schooling. He obtained only a grade-school education.

Around the time Samuel Morse was attending Yale College, Charles Goodyear first took notice of a piece of natural rubber, called gum elastic. "[While] yet a schoolboy," Charles said in his autobiography, in which he referred to himself in the third-person,

> *the wonderful and mysterious properties of this substance attracted his attention, and made a strong impression on his mind. A thin scale, peeled from a bottle or a shoe [came under his notice], and suggested to him that this would be very useful as a fabric, if it could be made uniformly so thin and could be so prepared as to prevent its adhering*

together and becoming a solid mass, as it soon did from the warmth and pressure of his hand.

Gum elastic was first brought to the United States in the early 1800s. Most of the first samples came from the sap, or gum, of certain tropical trees in South America. The gum was called elastic because it stretched when pulled. The word *rubber* came into usage because pencil marks could be erased by rubbing them with the material. There were several problems with the substance, however. In the winter, the rubber became hard as metal. In the summer, it became sticky and smelly. Hubert Terry in *India-Rubber and Its Manufacture* wrote, "India-rubber . . . is a tasteless opaque white substance having a more or less pronounced odour . . . the odour of rotten cheese . . . At temperatures below the freezing point India-rubber loses its elasticity, becoming quite rigid . . . At higher temperatures it becomes increasingly soft and plastic until . . . it melts into a sticky mass which cannot again assume the form and characteristics of the original substance."

Goodyear was soon too busy to give further thought to rubber. By the age of 17, he was in Philadelphia working as an apprentice with Rogers & Brothers to learn the hardware trade. Four years later, he returned to Connecticut to work as his father's business partner.

About this time, his father invented a steel farming fork for handling hay, and Charles witnessed some of the trials that an inventor faces. Although the invention was light and strong, many farmers hesitated to exchange their wrought-iron pitchforks for the steel ones. His father gave some of the steel forks away for free and after reports of excellent results, the steel forks sold easily.

Although he stayed away from machines that seemed complicated, Charles shared his father's interest in enhancing simple tools. "I have taken great satisfaction in trying to improve articles of necessity or convenience," Goodyear wrote.

On August 24, 1824, Charles married Clarissa Beecher, a member of the same church congregation. Their first child, Ellen, was born in July 1825.

In 1826, Goodyear opened a hardware store in Philadelphia. He obtained his supplies on credit and extended credit freely to his customers, too. Instead of paying for the items right away, Goodyear and his customers promised to pay their debts in the future. But too much credit and too little cash soon got Goodyear in trouble. The time came when his suppliers wanted cash payments.

Goodyear was given an extended time to fulfill his financial obligations, but he was unable to obtain enough cash from his customers to do so. By 1830, he had to sell his store. Even the proceeds from this sale were not enough to settle all his debts.

By this time, the Goodyears had three young children. Cynthia had been born in 1827 and Sarah in 1830. Goodyear was out of business and heavily in debt. He had few other prospects and was considered a poor credit risk. Goodyear became sick with worry and remained sickly nearly all his life.

His creditors took him to court. As partial punishment, Goodyear was sent to debtor's prison for part of a year. As each creditor made his claim over time, Goodyear was in and out of jail for the following 10 years.

His heavy debts and loss of credit prevented him from forming a new business. Learning a new occupation as an apprentice was commonly a job open only to teenagers. With his choices so limited, Goodyear turned to inventing. To invent something useful was the only way he knew to relieve his situation. Goodyear worked on inventions even while in his cell. In his first five years of effort, Goodyear received patents for a specially designed button, water faucet, and air pump.

During one of the times he was out of jail, in 1834, Charles visited a company's showroom in New York to see their life preservers. He was always interested in inventions that could save lives. On inspecting the company's life preserver, Goodyear saw a way to improve its air valve. After several weeks of tests, he came back to show his improvement to the store's sales agent.

This store happened to be owned by the Roxbury India Rubber Company. Gum elastic was also called India rubber because it had first been found by the Indians of South America and was also thought to come from the West Indies. Impressed with Goodyear's ingenuity, the sales agent explained that the company had a greater need for a more essential invention. If the changing properties of rubber could not be stabilized, the company as well as the entire rubber industry, was doomed.

Customers were returning their rubber goods and complaining about the poor quality. In cold weather, rubber coats stood stiff as boards; in the summer, rubber boots smelled so bad that people buried them underground. If an inventor created a rubber that kept its best qualities in all kinds of weather, the business would grow again, and the inventor would be amply rewarded. So far, however, all attempts to significantly improve rubber had failed.

Charles Goodyear

Although everyone else had given up, Goodyear grew enthusiastic. Sensible people said the stuff was useless. Goodyear, however, imagined new, wonderful possibilities for the substance. He focused on the good attributes the gum already had.

According to Goodyear:

The most remarkable quality of this gum is its remarkable elasticity . . . It can be extended to eight times its ordinary length, without breaking, when it will again resume its original form . . . the properties . . . excite in the human mind, when first called to examine it, an equal amount of curiosity, surprise, and admiration. Who can examine and reflect upon this property of gum elastic without adoring the wisdom of the Creator?

Goodyear returned home to Philadelphia eager to solve the rubber problem. At this time, however, another debt problem led him to be sent to jail again. Goodyear set up his first chemical laboratory in his cell. If he couldn't find employment outside prison, at least he could employ himself inside.

Although he was poor, Goodyear could afford some rubber samples and a few containers of chemicals. The gooey gum was cheap because no one wanted it. With little else to do, Goodyear worked day after day trying one experiment after another. At first, his only tools for getting the gum into shape were his fingers and a rolling pin.

After countless tries, Goodyear finally achieved some success. He found that half a pound of magnesium oxide (a white powder often called magnesia), when mixed with a pound of the gum, formed a compound that seemed to avoid stickiness in the sunshine.

The elated Goodyear hoped to go into rubber manufacturing and solve his credit concerns. At this time, Ralph B. Steele, a New Haven investor, came to Goodyear's rescue. He gave some capital to Goodyear to start his enterprise.

Free from jail, Goodyear obtained a cottage in New Haven for his new home and workshop and gathered his family. His wife and children were happy to be with him once again. The time since the hardware store failure had been tough for them, as well.

The children had spent the previous five years in poverty and rarely saw their father. They experienced severe childhood illnesses. By late 1835, Ellen was 10 and Cynthia eight, and baby William was a newborn. But baby Clarissa had lived less than a year when she died in 1831 and little Sarah had died in 1833. Charles, Jr., was almost three, having been born in January 1833. Ellen was left in charge while her mother visited Goodyear almost every day that he was in jail.

There would be more ordeals ahead, but some of the children would grow up to be successful in spite of the difficulties they faced.

For now, however, things were looking up for Goodyear. He hired some women to make hundreds of pairs of shoes and two workmen to help him build rubber lifeboats, made lighter with tubes of tin. Goodyear was happily running his own business again.

Goodyear changed the cottage kitchen into a workshop. He sat there for hours, working the gum with his hands. Even Ellen and Cynthia, as well as their mother, helped Charles with his chore. Strips of the new rubber were spread on dinner plates and windows. The pieces were peeled off after they dried. One of the first articles made was a purse that Ellen took to school. Her teacher commended the Goodyears on their fine handiwork.

In the autumn of 1835, Goodyear won medals at the fairs of the Mechanics' and American Institutes for his rubber goods. Professor Gale of New York University, the same man to help Samuel Morse with his telegraph, signed a certificate saying how well the gum was improved.

By early 1836, the first lot of Goodyear's new rubber shoes was completed. The shoes were beautifully made, but, after a season of exposure to warm weather, the gum softened and sagged.

Goodyear was exceedingly hopeful that he could prevent the softening, but his friends were not as sure. "They now became," Goodyear wrote in his autobiography, "entirely discouraged, and declined rendering him further assistance for such purposes, and those who had afforded his family supplies signified that they could do so no longer."

Goodyear had to sell all his furniture to cover his expenses. After moving his family to a cheap boardinghouse in the country, he deposited the family linen, hand-spun by his wife, as security for the rent he was unable to pay for the New Haven cottage. He hoped to earn some money soon so he could retrieve the linen. After some time, however, the linen was sold at an auction.

The family had almost nothing left. Their woes worsened when Charles, Jr., and William became very sick. Three-year-old Charles survived, but his little brother died.

Impoverished once again, Goodyear needed to do something soon. Two friends in New York came to his aid. One gave him a room to continue his tests on the gum; the other, a chemist, supplied him with the chemicals he required.

Goodyear took advantage of the opportunity. Others had given up on the gum, but not Charles Goodyear. By this time, the entire American rubber industry was disappearing. Stores were closing and warehouses stood empty. In fact, businesses of all kinds were on the brink of failure. The financial Panic of 1837 was beginning.

Goodyear's friend, William DeForest, came to visit him in his little room in New York. The worn, sickly Goodyear climbed the three flights of stairs, opened the door, and showed him the studio crammed with gum and chemicals.

William DeForest later related the story of this visit. "Here is something that will pay all my debts and make us comfortable," he recalled Goodyear saying. DeForest was not impressed. He told Goodyear the India rubber business was vanishing. Goodyear was still completely confident. He proudly pulled a piece of white rubber from his pocket and said, "And I am the man to bring it back again!"

For the following four years, Goodyear tried one chemical formula after another. He created several articles of rubber clothing and wore samples everyday to see how they held up in all kinds of weather. Goodyear told the story of what a gentleman in the city said when he was asked how to recognize Goodyear. He said, "If you meet a man who has on an India rubber cap, stock, coat, vest and shoes, with an India rubber money purse, without a cent of money in it, that is he."

The family fared little better than the father. There were times when Goodyear's brother Robert helped the family eat by fishing. Goodyear's family even wore some of his rubber as clothes. Clarissa Goodyear made rubber bonnets for the girls to wear to church. Then in 1838, the Goodyears had another baby. He was named William, like his brother before him.

Goodyear always felt that he was on the verge of the great answer. Just one more test, just one more hour, or one more week, and he would have it. Week after week went by. On several occasions, he informed his family and friends of his great discoveries. After further testing, however, the rubber refused to respond in some way or other. He moved his family to Massachusetts to be near the Roxbury company's rubber factory. Then, in early 1839, he found the solution.

A sample of his rubber, composed of his most recent chemical formula, came in contact with a hot stove. The natural gum always softened in summer heat. With the extreme heat of the stove, the gum should have melted. Instead of softening, however, Goodyear's newest rubber charred like leather. It could still stretch but it wasn't soft and sticky! Goodyear noticed that the edge of his sample was perfectly cured and not charred. If he could find the correct temperature, he could make fully cured rubber.

Goodyear eagerly showed the sample to his brother and friends. They were not interested. Goodyear had worn them out. He was treated like the boy in the children's story who cried wolf too many times when there wasn't one there.

This time, Goodyear *knew* he had the answer. The key seemed to be combining high temperature with the gum and sulfur. This new treatment would become known as *vulcanization*. To test his idea, Goodyear placed plain gum in boiling sulfur. This heat would normally melt the gum, but in the sulfur it charred. Like leather, the new rubber sample stayed in shape. It remained flexible in cold and warm temperatures.

Charles Goodyear. Artist's conception by George Rapp.
(Goodyear Tire and Rubber Co.)

Charles Goodyear

The rubber business could boom again! Thousands of new products could be created. Goodyear only had to get some funds, complete his tests, and the industry would soon be saved.

However, it was not going to be this easy. Too much time had passed. The old rubber industry was almost entirely out of business. Two full years lay ahead before a single person outside the family would listen to him. On his own, without funds, Goodyear renewed his experiments.

Goodyear soon found that there were several other variables to consider. These included time, composition, chemical quality, and heating techniques. Longer heating times led to firmer rubber. Charles found that adding white lead to the sulfur helped the curing process. The sulfur and white lead had to be completely dry. The best results usually occurred at 270° Fahrenheit, a temperature higher than the boiling point of water. The temperature had to be raised slowly and evenly.

These tests took time. Finding funds took time. The first two years were the toughest. The Goodyear family was often sick and without money for food or fuel. They foraged in fields to find wood for the winter. The children dug half-grown potatoes out of their garden for lack of anything else to eat.

Day by day, Goodyear borrowed for his family's survival. He made small requests for a cup of tea, or a pint of milk, or a bit of food. Sometimes he sold a few rubber articles or offered them as security for loans. The food often went to his family but the money went to his invention. Many people were critical of Goodyear for the way he was taking care of his family but he was too much in love with his invention to give up. Goodyear felt so close to success that he even sold his children's schoolbooks, after selling all of his own books, to get the few more dollars he felt he needed.

Although some people thought he was crazy, Goodyear eventually found a few supporters. He received generous help from Professor Benjamin Silliman, of Yale College, the chemistry teacher of Samuel Morse. On October 14, 1839, Silliman wrote this endorsement of Goodyear:

Having seen experiments made, and also performed them myself, with the India Rubber prepared by Mr. Charles Goodyear, I can state that it does not melt, but rather chars by heat, and that it does not stiffen by cold, but retains its flexibility in the cold, even when laid between cakes of ice.

Charles also received help from Oliver Coolidge, a friend of the family, who lent money for Goodyear's efforts and for his family's support. His family was helped by neighbors and relatives. Even his relatives, however, had a limited amount of food and money.

In 1840, Charles's wife was confined to her bed with baby Clarissa, born on May 12 and given the same name as her sister before her. At this time, two-year-old William became very sick. In a few days, William died. Goodyear had no money for a coffin or a carriage. For the funeral, the Goodyears walked sadly to the grave carrying the child in a wagon. The family was starving. Someone they didn't even know heard of their plight and sent them a whole barrel of flour, so they could have bread to eat.

Goodyear wrote to his old friend, William DeForest, a wool manufacturer and future brother-in-law (he would marry Goodyear's only sister Harriet). DeForest lent Goodyear enough money to take care of his family and allow him to travel to New York to try to interest some investors in his invention. Fortunately, his trip was successful. From this time on, Goodyear's family would not starve again.

In New York, Goodyear met the brothers William and Emory Rider. They were impressed with his samples and agreed to provide capital to carry on the new rubber enterprise. The greatest financial support, however, continued to come from William DeForest. Production was begun, and many rubber products started to sell.

In 1844, Goodyear received the patent for his vulcanization process. Charles wanted to spend his time on additional rubber inventions so he stayed out of the major manufacturing end of the rubber business.

Some of the new rubber items he made included life-saving boats and life preservers. He wanted every chair and couch on a boat to be usable as life preservers. Saving lives was often in the mind of this father who had lost so many children to illness.

Several companies honored licenses from Goodyear to make rubber products using his methods. Some did not. These other companies copied Goodyear's process without paying royalty fees. Goodyear had to get involved in lawsuits to protect his rights.

One of his cases, in 1852, was defended by Daniel Webster, a famous orator, lawyer, and politician. Goodyear had to cut short his first European trip, begun in 1851, to appear in court. Webster was defending the exclusive rights granted by the United States to Charles Goodyear in the form of his patent. Webster won this

*Charles Goodyear's rubber covered book can be seen
in the upper center. A lady's jeweled watch chatelaine
with a hard rubber cover is in the lower center.*
(Goodyear Tire and Rubber Co.)

lawsuit, commonly called The Great India Rubber Case. The claims made by others to his invention were dismissed. Goodyear then returned to Europe, celebrating his success with extravagant expenditures on his exhibitions. His excessive spending led to his final jail term, in Paris at the end of 1855.

After serving his sentence, Goodyear returned to the United States where his financial condition started to improve. Goodyear bought his first house in 1859 in Washington, D.C. He set up a workshop in the house with a pool for testing his life-preserver inventions. He was not able to enjoy this comfort long. He died on July 1, 1860, in New York City, soon after traveling by steamship to visit his sick daughter Cynthia, who died that same year.

Two of the children who survived him achieved notable success. Clarissa and Charles Goodyear's last child was born in 1846. Named William, after two of his brothers before him, he grew up to become a professor and a curator of a New York museum. His older brother Charles became a successful businessman in the rubber shoe business and invented improved shoemaking machines.

Charles Goodyear is acknowledged as the inventor of vulcanized rubber. In his honor, many rubber companies used the name Goodyear as part of their company name. Although founded after Goodyear's death, one of the most famous ones is the Goodyear Tire & Rubber Company.

By the 20th century, the rubber industry was employing almost a hundred thousand workers around the world creating millions of rubber products. One of the significant creations, of the thousands made possible by the vulcanized rubber process, was air-filled tires. Goodyear's process made the transportation vehicles of the 20th century possible.

The commissioner of patents of the United States at the time, Joseph Holt, said, "With such a record of toil, of privation, of courage, and of perseverance in the midst of discouragements the most depressing, it is safe to affirm that [Goodyear's] . . . diligence has been without parallel in the annals of invention."

Goodyear wrote of himself and other inventors,

It is often reported that "necessity is the mother of invention." It may with equal truth be said that inventors are the children of misfortune and want . . . There is, however, . . . an alleviating and controlling reflection . . . which is this: success has crowned their efforts to do that which they attempted, and they can leave the world better off for their having lived in it.

Chronology

December 29, 1800	Charles Goodyear is born in New Haven, Connecticut
1834	visits life preserver showroom; begins work on improving rubber
1839	vulcanizes a section of rubber for the first time
July 1, 1860	dies in New York City

Further Reading

Goodyear, Charles. *Gum, Elastic and Its Varieties with a Detailed Account of Its Applications and Uses, and of the Discovery of Vulcanization.* Volume I. New Haven: n.p. 1853. Includes autobiographical information. This book, and its companion volume, are not easy to find, but they are very useful and informative.

Goodyear, Charles. *The Application and Uses of Vulcanized Gum-Elastic; with Descriptions and Directions for Manufacturing Purposes.* Volume II. New Haven: n.p. 1853. The companion volume to Goodyear's first book. Describes the vast multitude of inventions and uses Goodyear envisioned for treated rubber. Full of illustrations.

Regli, Adolph Casper. *Rubber's Goodyear: The Story of a Man's Perseverance.* Illustrated by George Annand. New York: Julian Messner, Inc., 1949. One of the better Goodyear biographies available for young adults.

Wolf, Ralph F. *India Rubber Man: The Story of Charles Goodyear.* Caldwell, Idaho: The Caxton Printers, 1939. Informative, but boastful.

Cyrus Hall McCormick
(1809–1884)

*Cyrus Hall McCormick in mid-career. Engraving
of a painting by Cabanol.*
(State Historical Society of Wisconsin, WHi[x3]36818)

*I*n the summer of 1831, in a remote village nestled in the hills of
Virginia, Cyrus Hall McCormick readied his first grain harvesting
machine for a field test. His family and the local farmers came to
see the show. They were curious. Would Cyrus's contraption
work?

From the time farming began several thousand years earlier,
only three tools had been invented that successfully helped in the
harvest season. These were the sickle, scythe, and cradle. The
sickle is a curved knife on a short handle that requires stooping

to the ground to cut each handful of grain. The scythe is a longer, more gently curving blade on a long handle, allowing the holder to cut grain while standing. The cradle has "fingers" of wood attached above the scythe to allow the heads of the grain to fall in the same direction for easier bundling into sheaves.

A laborer could commonly harvest only a half-acre per day with the sickle and one to two acres with the scythe or cradle. Grain is ripe for harvesting for only a few days of the summer. Farmers and their families worked 12 hours or more a day to harvest the grain. They were lucky if they gathered enough grain to live on for the year. The labor was hard, but the cost of not working was starvation.

In the early 1800s, after centuries of farming experience, close to 90 percent of the occupations in America and the rest of the world were still focused on food production. This condition was likely to stay the same unless something was changed. Could that change come about as a consequence of the efforts of 22-year-old McCormick?

The answer would prove to be yes. McCormick's contraption worked and continued, in improved forms, to work into the current century. His horse-pulled contrivance cut six acres of oats that afternoon on the field of John Steele. Soon, his machine was cutting 12 acres a day. This increase meant that more grain could be harvested, in less time with less labor, resulting in cheaper and more abundant bread. Such a gain in yield was truly astounding.

Cyrus Hall McCormick was born on February 15, 1809, on a farm called Walnut Grove, in Virginia, the son of Robert and Mary Ann Hall McCormick. Cyrus gained a sibling every couple of years or so. He was followed by Robert, Susan, William, Mary Caroline, Leander, John, and Amanda.

Walnut Grove was among a community of farms that was almost 20 miles from the nearest town. Cyrus's first house was made of logs, although larger than the cabin Abraham Lincoln was born in three days earlier in the neighboring state of Kentucky. Like other local farm children, Cyrus obtained only a grade-school education at the Old Field School.

Along with his farm chores, Cyrus played with his seven younger brothers and sisters and enjoyed riding horses. He gained a reputation as a skillful rider. Cyrus led his church in song for several years and also enjoyed playing the fiddle. There was one other significant skill he acquired, and that was inventing. He learned about inventing from his father.

Besides being a farmer, Robert McCormick was an accomplished inventor. He created a grain threshing machine as well as several other types of farming equipment.

Cyrus made the first of his own inventions when he was a teenager. He constructed a smaller, lighter-weight cradle to make the work easier in the fields. He also invented a hillside plow, patented in 1831, and a "self-sharpening" plow, patented in 1833. On the farm, Cyrus was surrounded by his father's two sawmills, two grist mills, smelting furnace, and blacksmith workshop. This workshop is where Cyrus built his harvesting machine.

His father thought of the idea first. In 1816, Robert McCormick constructed a machine of a vastly different design than Cyrus would eventually develop. Revolving rods that turned with the forward motion of the ground wheels would catch the grain and whirl it across a row of short sickles. The grain nearly always tangled. He continued to try for 15 years before he gave up. Then Cyrus took his turn at the project.

Cyrus didn't know that there were others in England and America also working on harvesting machines at the same time. They developed various designs, but like Robert McCormick's, they didn't function well enough to be successful. Most successful inventions are enhancements or improvements of previous inventions that were inadequate. Cyrus had only his father's example to follow. "Having closely watched the operation of my father's machine," Cyrus later wrote, "I applied myself to the study of the principles and difficulties so far demonstrated."

Cyrus proceeded with an entirely new approach. He designed a divider so that the grain to be cut would be separated from the other grain, a large reel to lift and straighten the grain, a row of "fingers" to hold the grain to be cut, a back and forward moving knife to cut the grain, a platform to catch the grain, and a driving-wheel to carry the weight and operate the knife and reel. Since the cutting and gathering of ripe grain is called reaping, his machine became known as the Virginia Reaper. He completed his first reaper in less than two months.

Cyrus said he encountered "innumerable difficulties" in these early times and that he was "often advised by [his] father and family to abandon it." Obstacles came often, and his efforts were challenged every step of the way.

Cyrus Hall McCormick

In 1832, Cyrus demonstrated his reaper before a hundred people near the county-seat town of Lexington. The field was sloping and uneven. Cyrus was humiliated when his machine acted erratically, and the crowd jeered at him. The owner of the field, John Ruff, ordered him to remove his contraption. Cyrus was saved when the neighboring farmer, William Taylor, who 20 years later became a member of Congress, let him try the reaper on his more level ground. The jeers changed to cheers when the crowd saw the reaper clear several acres. That summer, Cyrus's reaper was exhibited in the courthouse square.

By the harvest of 1833, Cyrus McCormick had cut the grain of several farms. Letters appeared in the Virginia *Farmer's Register*. Archibald Walker wrote, "I certify that, having used one of Mr. McCormick's Reaping Machines on my farm, I can assert that the Machine performs well on level, and on steep land which is smooth, and that it will cut one acre per hour." James McDowell said, "I certify that Mr. McCormick's Reaping Machine, with a horse, was employed by me in the late harvest, and . . . I was

Summer harvest time. A McCormick self-rake reaper can be seen on the left and top center. A mowing machine is in use on the right.
(State Historical Society of Wisconsin, WHi[x3]33685)

satisfied with its work." John Weir wrote, "I have seen Mr. Cyrus H. McCormick's Grain-cutting Machine in operation for two seasons—it cut for me this season. I think it will perform well where the ground is clear of rocks and stumps; and will be a great saving of hand labor . . . I think it will cut about twelve acres per day, by being well attended."

With these early signs of success, McCormick allowed himself to dream of his future. He considered that he might someday make a million dollars. "This thought was so enormous that it seemed like a dream-like dwelling in the clouds—so remote, so unattainable, so exalted, so visionary," McCormick wrote. In an era when laborers worked for a nickel an hour, his goal seemed a fantasy.

Cyrus McCormick chose achievement in invention and manufacturing as his mission. He gave himself little time for frivolities or even romance. In a letter to a cousin, he wrote, "Mr. Hart has two fine daughters, right pretty, very smart, and as rich probably as you would wish; but alas! I have other business to attend to."

His visions of success seemed premature, however. The farmers came to look at his machine, but not to buy one. Common attitudes were that it was "a right curious sort of thing," and, "It's a wonderful contraption for stunts, but I'm running a farm, not a circus."

Feeling that his machine was not up to the standards of the community or even to his own, McCormick turned his attention to the farm he was given by his father and to an iron works idea. On the side, he continued to improve his reaper.

McCormick attended to his farm in 1835. He found that farming was not sufficiently stimulating as a sole occupation. As his sister Mary Caroline said in an interview, Cyrus simply "never liked to work on the farm. I remember when I was about twelve his saying that he had a great desire to be rich, not liking the life of a farmer."

So, "In 1836, full of enterprise and not satisfied to rest on my oars nor on my inventions," McCormick wrote, "an opportunity was presented to me to engage in the iron business . . . The dignity and position of an ironmaster was somewhat enviable." The iron business was considered to be a more profitable enterprise than farming.

With his father's participation and the help of some hired laborers, McCormick soon had an iron ore furnace ready for operation. For the next five years, however, McCormick's enterprise suffered a series of setbacks. Difficulties with falling iron prices, business partners, laborers, weather, bookkeeping, transportation, supplies, and financial obligations almost overcame him.

Cyrus and his father tried to outlast the hard times by acquiring funds on credit. Their debts eventually forced them to sell their business for a loss in 1841. Cyrus had to give up his farm, too. He nearly lost everything, except for his invention. This bleak situation strengthened McCormick's resolve to commit his energies solely on his reaper.

McCormick later wrote,

This [my iron work experiences] I have ever since felt to be one of the best lessons of my business experience. If I had succeeded in the iron enterprise I would perhaps never have had sufficient determination and perseverance in the pursuit of my reaper enterprise to have brought it to the present stage of success.

By necessity, McCormick looked to his invention as the way to salvage his career and to repay the debts he incurred in the iron business. He concentrated on his reapers and sold seven of them in 1842. McCormick announced in the Virginia *Richmond Enquirer* that "for some time to come, he intends to devote his attention exclusively to introducing his machines in different parts of the country . . . and will continue to have them manufactured in the best manner . . . guaranteeing their performance in every respect." Using his father's workshop as his manufacturing facility, McCormick sold 29 reapers in 1843, more than 50 in 1844, and more than 100 in 1845. All the creditors of the iron business were repaid by the following year.

Climbing out of debt was only one of the challenges that McCormick faced during this time. The second one came from his chief competitor, a one-eyed sailor named Obed Hussey. McCormick first became aware of Hussey when he saw a description of Hussey's invention in the *Mechanics' Magazine* of April 1834. It was of a different design but there were some similarities to McCormick's reaper. McCormick wrote a letter to the editor of the magazine attesting to his priority of invention on May 20, 1834. While the issue of reaper rights would eventually be contested in the courts, the competition continued to grow.

At first, Hussey's sales grew faster than McCormick's. Then in 1843, Hussey challenged McCormick to a contest. McCormick accepted. It rained during their first trial, near Richmond. Hussey's machine wouldn't cut the wet grain, while McCormick's was successful. In their second contest, McCormick's reaper cut 17 acres while Hussey's harvested only two. Hussey said he would bring his larger reaper. In this third contest, McCormick cut more than 12 acres while Hussey's machine broke down on the first try in tangled wheat. Hussey sold only two reapers that year, while McCormick sold 29. McCormick's sales forged ahead, and he was selling more than 1,500 reapers a year by 1850.

As his invention's popularity increased, McCormick tried allowing other manufacturers to build his reaper under license but found their quality less than equal to his high standards. In the mid-1840s, he toured other states by stagecoach and horseback, looking at farmlands and considering where to locate his own factory. When he came to Illinois, he saw farms of great size growing more grain than could be harvested. McCormick saw opportunity for his invention. He decided to establish his factory there to be close to his future customers. In 1848, he built a new facility in the town of Chicago. While the other competitors stayed in the established East, McCormick boldly moved to the wide Midwest where he expected the labor-light and land-laden farmers to be his best customers. He proved to be correct, and Chicago grew to be the trading and transportation center of the region. McCormick's company grew as Chicago grew. Chicago expanded from a town of 10,000 people in the 1840s to a city of over 100,000 by the end of the 1850s. The McCormick factory floor increased from the original 9,000 square feet in 1848 to 110,000 by 1859.

Just as McCormick revolutionized farming, he revolutionized business, as well. He evolved from a grade-school educated farmer's son to an inventor to a skilled business executive. His company organization grew well beyond the centuries-old tradition of an artisan and a few apprentices. McCormick was one of the earliest executives to institute modern ways of doing business that became standard. He assigned regions of the United States as sales territories and assigned sales supervisors to these areas. He hired traveling sales agents and repair personnel to meet the customer at the "field" site. He built interchangeable parts that could be ordered by mail and included customer testimonials and product guarantees in advertising. He also extended credit to his customers on a "use now, pay later" plan.

As his company expanded, so, too, did McCormick's view. He looked to Europe for further growth and, in 1851, he exhibited his invention at the Crystal Palace exhibition in London. As in the United States, recognition for his invention was not won easily.

Cyrus Hall McCormick

"A cross between a flying machine, a wheelbarrow and an Astley chariot [horse carriage]," the *London Times* said after seeing his invention. Other countries displayed precious jewels, silks, paintings, statues, and other renowned works of art. The sparse American display area of odd-looking contrivances was nicknamed "the prairie ground" and scoffed at by the English press.

In order to show the value of the inventions, the reapers on exhibit were given a field test on an English farm. Once again, McCormick's invention was matched against Obed Hussey's. The contest was held on a rainy day on wheat that was not fully ripe. There were almost 200 spectators, including a lord and a prince. Hussey's machine soon clogged up while McCormick's sped along, reaping well, at a speed estimated at 20 acres a day. The change in attitudes about McCormick's invention came swiftly.

The American editor Horace Greeley saw the contest and wrote,

It came into the field to confront a tribunal already prepared for its condemnation. Before it stood John Bull [England]— . . . his judgement made up and his sentence ready to be recorded. There was a moment, and but a moment, of suspense; then human prejudice could hold out no longer; and burst after burst of involuntary cheers from the whole crowd proclaimed the triumph of the Yankee Reaper. In seventy seconds McCormick had become famous. He was the lion of the hour; and had he brought five hundred Reapers with him, he could have sold them all.

"You can't imagine how the tone is altered," the American exhibit judge, B. P. Johnson, wrote to the *Albany Cultivator* in New York. "'The Prairie Ground' of America is now thronged. McCormick's machine is put back in its place and I believe yesterday more visited it than the Kohinoor diamond itself."

A second test on dry, ripe grain was given two weeks later, and McCormick's reaper won again. His invention was awarded a Grand Council Medal. The *London Times* now gave recognition and approval. "The Reaping machine from the United States," wrote the editor, "is the most valuable contribution from abroad . . . It is worth the whole cost of the Exhibition."

Cyrus collected other awards across Europe, including decorations from the French and Austrian emperors and gold medals from Germany. Success for McCormick and his invention became widespread.

The value of his reaper became so evident that scores of imitators sprang up. When McCormick filed for patent protection and extensions, as other inventors had been granted, the competitors hired the best lawyers they could find to represent them against McCormick. These lawyers included Abraham Lincoln, Stephen A. Douglas, and Edwin M. Stanton, among others. McCormick seldom won these cases and the number of competitors grew.

Yet, even in the increasingly competitive environment, McCormick's company continued to grow. By 1857, his company's sales increased to over $500,000 a year with costs, including labor and materials, totaling less than $200,000. McCormick was well on his way to his youthful dream of obtaining a million dollars. He was to achieve it by the end of the 1850s.

In 1857, seeing that his goals of success and financial security were well in hand, McCormick allowed himself time for other considerations. In June, Cyrus was introduced to Nancy (Nettie) Fowler, a lovely, intelligent, and single 22-year-old woman. Only two years before, a friend wrote to Cyrus's brother William that "the last time I saw him [Cyrus] at Washington the women were in full cry after him. He thought the dear angels wanted his money and ran the other way as fast as they pursued." This time, Cyrus initiated the pursuit.

On January 26, 1858, he and Nettie were married. More than 500 guests arrived at Cyrus's brother William's house for the reception. Cyrus provided for the food and other entertainment expenses. "It *must* be a splendid affair, if at all!" he said.

Life was good for McCormick. He succeeded in his dearest goals and became a renowned public personage. In 1860, his portrait was requested for a large canvas portraying the leading inventors of the United States. He wrote, "It may be proper for the artist to know . . . that my hair is a very dark brown,—eyes dark, . . . complexion fresh and health good, 5 ft. 11 1/2 inc. high, weighing 200 lbs. I prefer my portrait taken with more of a front face, if consistent with the position assigned me in the painting and would send you a likeness if wanted." McCormick's wish was fulfilled. Of the 20 inventors in the painting, *Men of Progress*, by Christian Schussele, McCormick is the only standing figure shown head to toe in a frontal position. A model of his reaper was also painted by his side.

In 1861, the Civil War began. Although he sympathized with some of the Southern economic and states' rights issues, McCormick declared his support of the Union when the war started. He said, "Though a native of the South, I am a citizen of Illinois, and of the United States, and as such shall bear true allegiance to

Cyrus Hall McCormick

Men of Progress. Engraving by John Sartain from Christian Schussele painting completed in 1862. Benjamin Franklin, can be seen overlooking the 19th-century inventors from his portrait on the upper left. Left to right: William Morton; James Bogardus; Samuel Colt; Cyrus Hall McCormick; Joseph Saxton; Charles Goodyear; Peter Cooper; Jordan Mott; Joseph Henry; Eliphalet Nott; John Ericsson; Frederick Sickels; Samuel F. B. Morse; Henry Burden; Richard Hoe; Erastus Bigelow; Isaiah Jennings; Thomas Blanchard; Elias Howe.
(National Portrait Gallery, Smithsonian Institution NPG.67.88)

the Government." McCormick's reaper helped the North win the war. While the sons of the farmers of the Midwest and East left to be soldiers in the Union armies, the new farm machinery replaced their missing labor. Even with fewer farm hands, food production increased to the highest levels of surplus ever known.

McCormick and hundreds of competitors produced over 125,000 reapers by 1861. By the end of the war, they would sell 250,000 more. The United States started to supply great quantities of grain to several other countries that were not able to produce sufficient food, including the empires of England and France. In November 1861, the U.S. ambassador to France, W. L. Dayton, wrote, "The bread of the North and West is an *absolute necessity* [to France]." America had to import wheat from other countries up until 1858. During the four-year span of the Civil War, the United States *exported* almost a quarter billion bushels of grain.

After the war, McCormick's company continued to thrive. He had survived the many obstacles of customer resistance, lack of capital, lack of business experience, business failure, lawsuits, loss of patent protection, intense competition, and even war. Now, his success reached new heights. By 1870, his factory was making about 10,000 harvesting machines a year.

Then came the Great Chicago Fire of 1871. Said to have started in the O'Learys' barn on DeKoven Street, this fire swept across Chicago like a stampede. Thousands of acres of the city's homes, stores, and factories were consumed and reduced to ashes and rubble. The McCormick Works factory was destroyed as well as its entire on-site inventory of almost 2,000 reaping machines.

Fortunately, McCormick's family was on vacation in Richfield Springs, New York, where he had left them to attend to his business in Chicago. His son Cyrus was 12, his daughters Mary Virginia and Anita were 10 and five. Cyrus was now 62. Should he retire or start all over again? He telegraphed a message to his wife that said, "All well . . . Could you all come here answer." After she came to his side in two days, "I at once determined to proceed with . . . rebuilding," he said in an address he wrote two years later.

McCormick chose to build an even larger facility on a new site in Chicago. Many of the farmers who had already received their reapers rushed payments in ahead of schedule to help McCormick and his company recover. Construction started in August 1872. Seven months later, the new factory began production.

From this time on, McCormick's company continued to be a success. He and his wife eventually had seven children, although two lived for only a short time. McCormick gave significant sums of money to his favorite churches and colleges. He was also given numerous awards and honors. In 1878 he was elected to the French Academy of Science, which said that he "had done more for the cause of agriculture than any other living man."

One of his earliest biographers, Herbert Casson, wrote that McCormick "truly represented the dawn of the industrial era [in America]—the grapple of the pioneer with the crudity of a new country, the replacing of muscle with machinery, and the establishment of better ways and better times in farm and city alike."

After an eventful life of 75 years, McCormick died at his home on May 13, 1884. That year, enough grain was shipped from

Cyrus Hall McCormick

Chicago (then a city of 600,000 people) to make 10 *billion* loaves of bread. His eldest son, Cyrus H. McCormick, was chosen as the new president of the McCormick Harvesting Machine Company. He would eventually merge the company with some of his competitors' to form the International Harvester Company, which became an industry giant in the 20th century. Soon, engine-powered combines, the successors to McCormick's invention, were harvesting up to 50 acres a day. One farmer could do the work that used to require a hundred laborers.

These considerable advances all sprang from the simplest beginnings of a country youth's effort in a rustic workshop on a farm in Virginia. McCormick's "contraption" led to increasing the food supply of the United States and the world. The coming industrial age, one of the greatest times of change in America, created new occupations and required workers to fill them. They came from the farm, thanks to the efforts of inventors such as Cyrus Hall McCormick.

Chronology

February 15, 1809	Cyrus Hall McCormick is born on Walnut Grove farm in Virginia
1831	demonstrates his first reaper invention on John Steele's field; patents hillside plow
1833	cuts the grain of several farms with the reaper; patents self-sharpening plow
1843	wins harvesting contest against Obed Hussey's reaper; sells 29 reapers
1870	starts making 10,000 harvesting machines a year
May 13, 1884	dies in Chicago

Further Reading

Judson, Clara Ingram. *Reaper Man: The Story of Cyrus Hall McCormick.* Boston: Houghton Mifflin Company, 1948. Has fictional conversations and imagined situations. Few recent young adult books on Cyrus Hall McCormick are available.

Hutchinson, William Thomas. *Cyrus Hall McCormick: Seed Time, 1809–1856.* New York and London: The Century Co., 1930. Volume 1. A thorough, detailed biography. Well-documented.

Hutchinson, William Thomas. *Cyrus Hall McCormick: Harvest, 1856–1884.* New York and London: D. Appleton-Century Co., 1935. Volume 2. A very thorough biography.

Roderick, Stella Virginia. *Nettie Fowler McCormick.* Rindge, New Hampshire: Richard R. Smith Publisher, Inc., 1956. Well-researched. Includes letters from inventor to his wife.

George Westinghouse (1846–1914)

George Westinghouse in 1906.
(Westinghouse Historical Collection,
Westinghouse Electric Corporation)

*I*n September 1868, George Westinghouse was working on his first train brakes. Westinghouse installed them on a four-car train for a demonstration of their effectiveness in Pittsburgh, Pennsylvania. They were called air brakes because they used compressed air, or air under pressure, to push the brakes against the train wheels. People were skeptical about the new brake. Westinghouse hoped this test would change their minds.

The judges and other invited guests climbed into the end car of the train along with Westinghouse. The engineer, Daniel Tate, started the locomotive and increased the train's speed to about 30 miles an hour. Before the train came to the first station, an accident occurred.

Up ahead, a cart driver decided he could get across the tracks ahead of the train. He was nearly across when his horse shied at the sound of his shout. He flipped off his wooden seat and landed on the track. The onrushing train came straight toward him.

Fortunately, the engineer saw the mishap and pulled on the handle next to him. The loud sound of scraping metal wheels whined in everyone's ears. The compressed air whooshed through the hoses between each car. The first car stopped first, then came the second, followed by the third, and finally the end car. With the first cars already slowed, the end car slammed into them, tossing all the guests, along with Westinghouse, out of their seats.

When the train stopped, the engineer rushed to the fallen man as he lay only feet away from the front of the giant locomotive. Westinghouse and his guests came out to see what had happened. After the man was helped to his feet and cared for, the significance of the event slowly dawned on everyone. The air brakes had saved the cart driver's life.

Earlier brakes had required passenger train brakemen to turn a separate hand wheel on every car of the train. A train was seldom stopped in time during an emergency. Even when entering a station, the train often skidded past the platform and had to be put in reverse. Westinghouse's invention gave control to the engineer in the front of the train and improved transportation safety.

Westinghouse created several other inventions, obtaining nearly 400 patents in his lifetime. Besides air brakes and engines, Westinghouse's contributions included signaling work, steam turbines, electrical systems, lighting, telephone switches and exchanges, natural gas equipment, and electric railways. His efforts also led to lighting the Chicago World's Fair of 1893 and building electric generators at Niagara Falls in 1895, some of the first public displays of alternating electric current in America.

George Westinghouse was born to George, Sr., and Emmeline Westinghouse in a village called Central Bridge in the countryside of New York on October 6, 1846. He grew up with three older brothers, three older sisters, and one younger brother. Two other brothers lived only a short time.

George Westinghouse

As a young child, George gained a reputation for temper tantrums. To get his way, he sometimes stamped his feet, screamed, or banged his head on the wall. These techniques did not always work. His older brothers liked to tease him, just to see what funny actions he would take. Years later, George learned gentler ways to get what he wanted, and nearly always succeeded.

George did not adjust well to the confinement and routine of school. He liked to live life his own way. His favorite activity was visiting his father's shop. If he was shooed away from there, he would play on the grass with wooden shapes of mechanical parts.

Although born a generation later, George enjoyed a boyhood similar to Cyrus Hall McCormick's. George's father was born in the same year as Cyrus and lived the same life span. The senior George had a shop on his farmland where he labored on grain-gathering inventions. Like Cyrus, young George watched his father work until he felt ready to create some inventions of his own.

In 1856, George's father moved the family to Schenectady, New York. After establishing a shop on the south bank of the Erie Canal, he built small steam engines and mill machinery as well as farming equipment. He hired other workers and had a sign saying "G. Westinghouse & Co." painted on the side of his shop.

George, Sr., included his sons in the company, too. First Jay, the eldest, was hired, followed by John, then Albert. George, Jr., started working for 50 cents a day, outside the school season, when he was 13. In the spring of 1862, at 15, he was promoted to a daily rate of 87 and a half cents.

Young George sometimes got in trouble with his father for working on little gadgets instead of the project he was assigned. One of the workmen set up a small workshop for George in the loft. After hours, George liked to stay up there constructing his own creations.

In 1861, the Civil War started. George's father tried to keep his sons out of the conflict, saying that it would be over soon. But, by the summer of 1862, the Confederate armies still seemed strong and George, Sr., changed his mind.

In August, Albert signed up for the volunteer cavalry. John followed him, getting a commission in the navy. In 1863, at 16, George signed up as a soldier and soon joined the cavalry, too. It was common for boys to enlist in the armed forces. About half the soldiers in the Civil War joined up when they were 18 or younger.

After some months of scouting duty, George changed from the army to the navy. On December 1, 1864, he was appointed an acting third assistant engineer. He served on the ship *Muscoota*, the *Stars and Stripes*, and with the Potomac fleet of smaller ships.

George Westinghouse, about 17, in a Civil War portrait.
(Westinghouse Historical Collection, Westinghouse
Electric Corporation)

George still found time to tinker on his inventions. One of his friends from the Schenectady shop lent him a lathe for shaping metal and wood. George kept it aboard ship to use during his off-duty hours.

George Westinghouse

In 1865, the Civil War ended. In September, George entered Union College as his father wished him to improve his education. As usual, George spent most of his time thinking about inventions instead of his studies.

For the last four years, George had tinkered on a steam engine of his own design. That year, his efforts bore their first fruit. On October 31, George Westinghouse received patent number 50,759 for his invention of a rotary steam engine.

After the Christmas holidays, Westinghouse left college to concentrate on his inventions. After some convincing, his father employed him at his shop again.

While on a business trip for his father in 1866, Westinghouse's train was delayed because two cars of the train ahead had come off the track. The enormous efforts of the crew to slowly inch the cars back onto the track inspired George to think of his second invention. To save time, the crew could have simply clamped two rails to the track at an angle to the wheels of each derailed car. Designing this idea as a separate item of railroad equipment, Westinghouse called his invention a car replacer. He obtained the patent on February 12, 1867.

To his surprise, Westinghouse received little support from his father when he asked for funds to sell the invention to the railroad companies. He thought George didn't know the railroad business very well and should stick to things he knew best. Set in his goal, Westinghouse decided he would learn everything he could on the subject and seek investors on his own.

That same year, he began improving railroad "frogs," the devices for keeping cars on the correct rails at intersections and track switches. The old iron ones kept wearing out. Westinghouse invented reversible frogs, so they could be turned over when one side became worn, and he made them of cast steel.

Train rides continued to provide inspiration for Westinghouse. While riding on the Hudson River Railroad on a trip from New York, he found a vacant seat in the last car of the crowded train. Next to him was Marguerite Erskine Walker.

Westinghouse started a conversation and learned she was on her way to visit relatives. Before she came to her station, Westinghouse asked to see her again. She expressed the proper hesitancy and modesty of the times, so Westinghouse wrote the names and addresses of several people who could answer questions on his character.

As soon as he reached Schenectady, Westinghouse talked to the minister of his church. He asked him to write a letter to Marguerite Walker explaining Westinghouse's standing in the community. When he came home that evening, Westinghouse announced to his family that he had met the woman he wanted to marry.

The eager Westinghouse visited Walker and her family several times. Before he was quite 21, George married Marguerite on August 8, 1867. They moved in with George's family until they could afford a house of their own.

Fortunately for Westinghouse, with the help of a steel manufacturer, his railroad frogs started to sell by the thousands. He received his first patent for them on April 7, 1868.

While on yet another train trip, George came up with the invention that would make him famous. Traveling from Schenectady to Troy, the train slowed to a stop before reaching the next station. Up ahead, two loaded freight trains had crashed in a head-on collision.

Westinghouse walked over to view the crew cleaning up the wreckage. Torn cargo, wood, and metal lay scattered all over the track. Fortunately, it was not a passenger train.

The hand brakes had been tried, but they could not stop the trains in time. Westinghouse wondered if an invention could be made to stop trains sooner. He wasn't the first to have this idea, but he was one of the few who chose to do something about it.

After reading about the use of compressed air in Europe for tunnel drilling, Westinghouse thought it might also be used for train brakes, too. If air under pressure could help drive giant holes through mountains, he decided it was strong enough to help stop moving trains. In July 1868, Westinghouse applied for his patent.

In his first design, a steam pump on the locomotive pushed compressed air into a tank under the floor. With the turn of a handle, a valve would open, allowing the air to race through pipes and hoses to all the cars of the train. Each car had its own set of braking equipment. As a cylinder under each car filled with air, a metal rod came out to apply the brakes to the wheels.

In September, Westinghouse tested his invention on the four-car train in Pittsburgh. He sent a telegraph message to his father, saying, "My air brake had practical trial today on passenger train . . . and proved a great success."

Improvements in brakes became especially important as train weights and speeds increased. Since 1830, dozens of American and British inventors had created brakes of all kinds, including hand, chain, spring, steam, vacuum, and compressed air. Westinghouse was one of the first to make a swift and strong system. Eventually, his designs became the American industry standard.

In July 1869, George organized the Westinghouse Air Brake Company. At first, the new brakes were slow to be accepted. Then, as reports of their sureness spread, sales increased substantially. Even before sales became significant, the confident Westinghouse moved to Pittsburgh and bought his first house and land.

His confidence continued. Eight railroads were using his brakes on less than 400 cars by September 1870. Four years later, the number of cars was over 7,000. Eventually, the number exceeded 100,000.

As the air brake became more common, Westinghouse worked on two weaknesses in his original design. The first involved the separation of cars. Once a car was disconnected from the locomotive, its brakes were useless. The second was the time it took for the air to reach the last cars in a train.

To solve these problems, Westinghouse came up with a new invention, the triple valve.

The triple valve attached to every car and performed three tasks. First, it accepted air from the train line into its own reserve tank. Its second job was to set the brake, which it did by filling the brake cylinder out of this separate tank. As the cylinder became filled, the air forced the brake out. Third, it let the air out of the cylinder to release the brake.

This way, each car had its own supply of compressed air immediately available. If the engineer released some of the air in the main train line or if there was a separation, the triple valve used its own air supply to set the brake on each car. When the engineer restored the air pressure, the triple valve released the brakes and returned to its original condition.

Westinghouse's company continued to grow. By 1883, over 50,000 cars were equipped with Westinghouse air brakes.

Year by year, train lengths and total tonnage increased to handle the growth of the country. As good brakes became essential, other inventors tried to enter into competition.

In 1886 and 1887, the Master Car Builders association had contests at Burlington, Iowa, to see who had the best brakes. The test trains had 50 cars. In the early tests, even Westinghouse's brakes did not perform well enough on a train of this length. The top time in 1886 for stopping the train was 22 seconds, and the end cars crashed into the ones in front.

In the 1887 contests, some new inventors, including Herman Hollerith, entered the field with electrically controlled brakes. To Westinghouse's alarm, the judging committee decided that air brakes actuated by electricity were the fastest method. At the time, however, electricity was not considered as reliable as compressed air, especially if the wires broke during train movement.

The stiff competition spurred Westinghouse to make even further improvements. He sped up the action in the air delivery and valves, shortening the stopping time first to six seconds, and then to an incredible 2½ seconds. This time proved sufficient to ensure continued growth to Westinghouse's company. Eventually, however, the company had to turn to electricity to stop high-speed trains in time.

One of the Burlington Brake Test 50-car trains used in 1887.
(Westinghouse Historical Collection, Westinghouse Electric Corporation)

By the 1880s, Westinghouse was involved in several enterprises. As well as the companies and patents he originated on his own, he also started purchasing the companies and patents of others, too. He seemed to find opportunities everywhere.

Among the early companies he formed or acquired were the Union Switch and Signal Company, the Philadelphia Company for handling natural gas, the Westinghouse Machine Company, and the Westinghouse Electric Company.

Although he became interested in many concerns, his fascination for electricity especially grew. With his experience in the railroad industry, Westinghouse learned to think big. The nation was filled with a vast track transportation system that brought goods more swiftly, safely, and cheaply than any other means at the time. Like Thomas Edison, Westinghouse conceived of a similar system of electricity, providing cheap and abundant power to every community in the country.

The two inventors shared the dream but differed in their approach. Westinghouse favored large alternating current generating stations that could send electricity long distances to several communities at once. Edison liked smaller direct current generating stations that serviced one community each.

An electrical generator can be explained by using a bar magnet and a coil of wire. Electricity is generated if the magnet is pulled through the coil, or if the coil is pulled across the magnet. They can be moved by hand, wind, steam, or other form of power. If the magnet or coil action is in one direction only, then direct current is produced in the wire. If the action is two-way, then the current will alternate in both directions. The number of times the coil or magnet is moved back and forth will determine the cycles per second speed of the alternating electrical current.

Edison based all his electrical inventions on the idea that they would use electric current that moved in one direction. Two-way alternating current was new and untested. To build a system based on alternating current would require combining the efforts of a large team of inventors and a large investment of funds and time. Westinghouse accepted this challenge. By acquiring the patent rights to the newest alternating current inventions of Europe and America with generous offers and hiring the best electrical experts available, Westinghouse strove to achieve his goal.

Among the contributors were John Gibbs and Lucian Gaulard who provided the transformers that could step up electrical power for long-distance service and also step it down to levels safe for homes and offices. The transformer equipment used the current in one coil of wire to induce an electric current in a second coil. If the second coil had more turns of wire than the first, then the electrical voltage would be stepped up. If the second coil had less, then the electricity would be stepped down. William Stanley improved both the transformer and the electrical generators.

Oliver Shallenberger invented the electric meter, and Nikola Tesla provided the electric motors.

By 1892, Westinghouse was ready to show what the alternating current system could do. Submitting the lowest bid, he won the contract to light up the Chicago World's Columbian Exhibition.

An interior section of the Electricity Building at the Chicago World's Fair of 1893. The Westinghouse electrical systems and Tesla motor were on display.
(Division of Electricity and Modern Physics, National Museum of American History, Smithsonian Institution, Negative no. 80-20135)

Almost all the top inventors of this century attended great exhibitions to show off their inventions. In its time, the Chicago World's Columbian Exhibition was considered as impressive as EPCOT Center in Walt Disney World in Florida and the multitude of Smithsonian museums in Washington, D.C., are today. Beautiful and elaborate fountains and waterways were surrounded by giant statues and immense exhibition halls built in the style of classical European architecture.

In the Midway, run by two 1,000 horsepower engines, stood the world's first gigantic ferris wheel. Between its two giant rings, rising over 26 stories to the sky, were 36 cars with room for 60 people in each.

One of the exhibition buildings was longer than five football fields and wider than two. The 12 electric generators, each the size of a locomotive, were housed in the nearby Machinery Hall. Of the several smaller structures, only 700 feet or so each, one was dedicated just to electrical exhibitions. Here, Westinghouse displayed some of his electrical equipment along with Tesla's motors.

Tesla's motor was so important a contribution that the electric generators were redesigned to accommodate it. *Two* electric currents were sent in each direction, one current a half-step behind the other, so the motor would run efficiently. The speed at which the current was sent back and forth was set to 60 cycles a second, still the U.S. standard for electricity. An agreed-upon speed allowed a household appliance to work anywhere in the country.

One of the greatest spectacles was the electric lighting of the fair. It was the best of its time. Edison's first direct current station, installed in New York City in 1882, lighted 400 lamps the first year. At the Chicago world's fair opening in the spring of 1893, Westinghouse's alternating current station gave electricity to 8,000 arc lights and 130,000 light bulbs. In case some of them needed to be changed, George had his lighting company make 250,000 lights for the occasion.

Due to the success of this installation and the expertise of his engineers, Westinghouse was awarded the contract for harnessing the power of Niagara Falls, for the first large-scale hydroelectric generating station in America.

By 1896, three 5,000-horsepower alternating current generators were operating on power from the falls. On November 16, the electricity was sent 20 miles away to light up the city of Buffalo, New York. Over time, the generating station would be expanded to service a large section of the state of New York. After all the work was done, the Niagara River still flowed over the falls as beautifully as it had for centuries.

The project set the standard for the future of electrical service in America. One of Westinghouse's chief engineers, Lewis Stillwell, wrote that the effects "were of vast importance—comparable . . . to the successful operation of the first steam locomotive." He gave special tribute to Westinghouse: "We all worked together with enthusiasm and harmony, directed and inspired by Mr. Westinghouse."

From this time forward, alternating current stations spread across the country, providing electricity to almost every community in America. Eventually, Edison agreed that the astonishing growth was made possible by the development of alternating current electricity.

Tesla later said in a speech,

George Westinghouse was in my opinion, the only man on the globe who could take [the] alternating current system under the circumstances then existing and win the battle against prejudice and money power. He was a pioneer of imposing stature and one of the world's noblemen.

George Westinghouse continued to expand his efforts in several areas, eventually founding 60 companies based on inventions. Inventive all his life, he obtained 61 of his 361 patents, mostly for engines and turbines, after he was 60 years old. He died on March 12, 1914, at the age of 67. He and Marguerite were survived by one child, born in 1884, named George, like his father and grandfather.

Westinghouse was well liked for his interest in his fellow inventors and the generous benefits he provided to the thousands of employees at his companies. He improved transportation safety, electrical services, and met several other requirements of the growing country.

Of all his accomplishments, Westinghouse simply said,

If someday they say of me that in my work I have contributed something to the welfare and happiness of my fellow men, I shall be satisfied.

Chronology

October 6, 1846	George Westinghouse is born in Central Bridge, New York
1864	appointed acting third assistant engineer for United States Navy
1865	receives first patent, for a rotary steam engine
1868	Westinghouse receives patent for railroad frogs; invents railroad air brake
1883	invents triple valve
1893	exhibits alternating current electrical system at Chicago World's Columbian Exhibition
1896	starts electrical power generation at Niagara Falls, New York
March 12, 1914	dies in New York City

Further Reading

Garbedian, Haig Gordon. *George Westinghouse: Fabulous Inventor*. With Photographic Supplement. New York: Dodd, Mead & Company, 1943. Has conjectured dialogue. Written for young adults.

Levine, I. E. *Inventive Wizard: George Westinghouse*. New York: Julian Messner, Inc., 1962. Has fictional dialogue but is well researched. Written for young adults.

Thomas Alva Edison
(1847–1931)

Thomas Alva Edison in 1904.
(National Museum of American History, Smithsonian
Institution, Negative no. 80, 16542)

As a teenager, Thomas Edison worked as a telegraph operator. Inspired by the telegraph, he tested all sorts of electrical creations of his own. By the time he was 21, Edison felt ready to patent his first invention.

Edison soon attracted the attention of the world. His efforts led to the creation of the phonograph as well as improvements to the telegraph, telephone, electric light, storage battery, electric generator, electric distribution system, ore-separator, prefabricated housing, and many other inventions.

Edison was eventually issued 1,093 patents from the United States Patent Office and over a thousand from foreign countries as well. This total is greater than that obtained by any other inventor *ever*.

Carrying a model of an invention he constructed of wood, Edison came to Washington, D.C., for the first time in 1868. On October 28, the patent for his first invention was filed at the Patent Office.

The shelves inside the four-winged building contained thousands of models created by inventors before Edison. Steamboats, reapers, telegraph instruments, and all sorts of other contrivances stood on display. Soon, Edison's own invention would be included in the collection.

Edison called his creation the electrical vote recorder. Edison said he was "struck with the enormous waste of time in Congress and in State legislatures by the taking of votes on any motion." With his new invention, the lawmakers could instantly vote with the press of a button and have their choices displayed on a record board. "This contrivance would save several hours of public time every day in the session," said Edison.

Some of Edison's friends had tried unsuccessfully to interest the state legislature of Massachusetts in his invention. Edison thought he would try the United States Congress, believing that they would see the importance of his invention.

Edison spoke to the head of a congressional committee. "I enthusiastically set forth its merits," said Edison in an interview. "Imagine my feelings when, in a horrified tone, he exclaimed: 'Young man, that won't do at all! That is just what we do *not* want.'"

The Congress did not want to change. They liked their voting process slow to allow some lawmakers time to stall the passage of laws they felt should not be approved. "I saw the force of his remarks," said Edison, "and was about as crushed as it was possible to be at my age."

Even though no one wanted his first invention, Edison decided to try again with a second one. From this time forward, however, he concentrated his efforts on creations certain to gain customer confidence. "Anything that won't sell I don't want to invent," Edison said in an early interview, "because anything that won't sell hasn't reached the acme [summit] of success."

Edison chose business owners and investors for his next customers. They eventually expressed great interest in Edison's inventive talents.

On January 25, 1869, Edison submitted his invention of a stock ticker for patent approval. This invention would enable owners and investors to see the value of their shares in a business printed on a strip of paper. Edison grew confident that he would soon succeed in a career of inventing. Five days later, *The Telegrapher* announced that Thomas A. Edison "would hereafter devote his full time to bringing out inventions."

Thomas Alva Edison was born to Samuel and Nancy Edison in the canal town of Milan, Ohio, on February 11, 1847. Called Al as a boy, Edison was the youngest child in his family. His sister Tannie (Harriet Ann) was older by 14 years, his brother William Pitt by 15, and his sister Marion by 17. As an infant, Al shared a room with Tannie and Pitt. Tannie liked to write and Pitt enjoyed drawing. In the future, Edison would fill his notebooks with words and sketches of ideas for inventions.

After he reached school age, young Edison lived like an only child. With his brother and sisters grown up, he often wandered about on his own. Always curious, his travels led him to the canal, grain elevators, barns, creeks, farm animals, farmers, canal boatmen, and townspeople.

Edison's earliest exposure to an inventor came at the shop of Sam Winchester, a flour mill owner who constructed a passenger balloon. Although Edison was impressed, the other townspeople thought Winchester was crazy. Eventually, Winchester floated in the sky toward Lake Erie and vanished. He had left the town for good.

Al's father owned a lumberyard and was fairly successful for awhile. Over time, however, the expanding railroads shifted trade away from Milan. The town economy grew poor, so Samuel Edison changed his place of business. In 1854, the Edisons moved to Port Huron, a town in Michigan by Lake Huron and Canada.

Like many other children of the time, Al received only a grade school education. His mother, a former schoolteacher, enhanced his education at home. She encouraged her son to study books of classic literature as well as science.

One of Edison's early science books was called *School of Natural Philosophy*, by R. G. Parker. This work showed scientific experiments that could be tested at home. Edison said this was "the first book in science I read when a boy, nine years old, the first I could understand."

Nancy Edison educated Al to the point where he could educate himself. He created his own laboratory in the cellar and soon completed all the experiments in his books. From then on, Edison conducted tests that couldn't be found in books.

Edison's early tests were not always successful. Sam Winchester's work with lighter-than-air gas to lift the giant balloon to the sky inspired Al to think of an interesting experiment. If a child were filled with gas, the child would be lighter than air, too, Al thought. He stirred a bubbling concoction of powders including baking soda in a glass of water. Then he gave some to a friend. Instead of flying, the other boy stayed on the ground with a stomachache. Eventually, Edison learned to be a little more careful with his experiments.

Edison constructed his first homemade telegraph set when he was 11. With his chemicals, he made his own batteries, too. Through the woods between two houses, Al built a telegraph line out of stove pipewire. To keep the wire off the ground, he laid the line across bottles pegged onto the trees. Edison said it worked fine.

When Edison was 12, the Grand Trunk Railroad connected tracks to Port Huron. Al loved the excitement of the steam locomotive and the handsome carriages it controlled. The railroad also used telegraph sets at each train station! Edison was one of the first to apply for the job of newsboy on the train.

After Al was selected, he came to his mother with the good news. She became concerned about her son's safety and education. Edison convinced her he would be careful and use the money he earned to help the family as well as buy books and science supplies to continue his education. She decided to show her faith in him and gave her approval. "My mother was the making of me," wrote Edison, "She was so true, so sure of me; and I felt that I had someone to live for, someone I must not disappoint."

Al took the job on the local shuttle train. It left Port Huron in the morning and came home from Detroit every evening. On the train, the boy sold newspapers along with sandwiches, fruits, and other items. Edison eagerly studied in a Detroit library for several hours while waiting for the return train in the late afternoon.

Besides science subjects, Edison enjoyed reading the books of Thomas Paine and Victor Hugo. Eventually, he taught himself to read very rapidly.

As he became friends with the train employees, the enthusiastic Edison was sometimes given special treatment. One of his favorite privileges came from the conductor of the train. He allowed Edison to keep a chemical laboratory in an unused section of the baggage car.

Thomas Alva Edison at age 14.
(National Museum of American History, Smithsonian Institution, Negative no. 80, 16555)

Al worked on this train for almost four years, selling newspapers and other goods and working in his traveling lab. As he grew into a teenager, he continued to obtain various laboratory supplies with his earnings and increase his knowledge of science.

At 15, Edison's luck changed one day when the train lurched on a section of track. Before he could catch it, a water-filled bottle containing a stick of phosphorous slipped from his storage shelf. Exposure to air caused the chemical to burst into flame as it crashed on the wooden floor. Fortunately, the conductor came with water and saved the car. At Smith's Creek station, the very next stop, the conductor threw Edison and his entire lab off the train. Although soon given his job on the train back, Al had to keep his chemicals at home.

The Mount Clemens station grew to have special significance to Edison. That same summer, the station became the scene of an event that affected Al's life. On a morning train run, Edison stood on the platform at the station with his newspapers. The station agent was in the telegraph office. Other people were occupied with their work and travel plans. They didn't see the three-year-old son of the station agent playing in the gravel, right in the path of a moving freight car. Luckily, Al saw the boy. Tossing his papers to the side, Edison raced to the track, grabbed the child, and carried him to a safe spot. The boxcar rolled across the place where the boy had been playing. Onlookers saw the rescue and cheered. The station agent was called out of the office. He came over to Edison and conveyed his deepest thanks.

In gratitude, the father, Jim Mackensie, offered to teach Al everything he knew about the telegraph as well as the special railroad sending codes. Mackensie knew the Edison family and was familiar with their son's interests. Edison eagerly accepted the offer. He trained on the telegraph for several weeks and found employment as a telegrapher that winter.

It is likely that Edison would have learned telegraphy eventually, even without having saved the child. In fact, he already knew Morse Code and had constructed his own telegraph instruments. But this event led to a special friendship between Edison and Mackensie. The elder Mackensie visited Edison frequently in his future laboratory.

From the ages of 16 to 20, Edison traveled across the central and southern United States as a telegrapher. He continued to buy electrical supplies for his experiments and read books in the town libraries. He designed electrical gadgets for making the telegraph work easier as well as electric shock plates for catching the cockroaches and rats at the rustic stations and hotels where he stayed. Some telegraphers thought Edison was clever; he told stories and played practical jokes. Others thought him odd; they made fun of Edison and his ideas.

Edison frequently got fired for spending time on his gadgets instead of attending to his duties. Then he would travel to the next county or state and start a new job. Edison would enter the station office, show off his lightning speed at the telegraph, and often get hired immediately. Fortunately for Edison, there were always new openings in the expanding telegraph business.

In 1868, after five years as a telegrapher, Edison awoke to the lack of future goals in his life when he read the works of the English electrical scientist Michael Faraday. Like Edison, Faraday had little schooling, educated himself, started with chemical experiments, and then moved into the electrical field. Faraday continued on to discover several laws of electromagnetism as well as electrochemistry. His finding that electric current could be induced by magnets formed the basis of the electric generator.

According to one of his best telegrapher friends, Edison said, "I am now twenty-one. I may live to be fifty. Can I get as much done as he did? I have got so much to do and life is so short, I am going to hustle."

Edison immediately tried to complete a telegraph set that would send messages in two directions at the same time. He had arrived in Boston in the spring of 1868 to work as a telegrapher for Western Union. Edison announced his invention efforts in a June telegraph journal. He continued to test his "double transmitter" for the telegraph while also creating a new invention. By October, Edison was ready to bring the electrical vote recorder to Washington.

After failing to interest Congress in his voting machine, Edison again concentrated on improving the telegraph. He set up his equipment in a section of an electrical shop owned by Charles Williams. This same shop of telegraph repair and custom invention construction was to be of service to Alexander Graham Bell a few years later.

After leaving his job as a telegrapher, Edison learned that success would not come easily. Simply announcing his intentions to be an inventor was not enough. Long days and nights of steady work still lay ahead.

In April 1869, Edison thought his duplex, or two-way, telegraph, was ready for demonstration. A successful show would attract investor financing for his enterprise. He set up a field test on a telegraph line from Rochester, New York, to New York City.

With investors looking on, Edison sent some code through his instrument in Rochester. Unfortunately, no message came from the operator at the other end of the line. After waiting some time for a reply, the investors lost interest and withdrew their support. Edison thought the operator just needed training, but it was too late. The show had failed.

With no income, Edison's financial situation grew grim. He decided to leave Boston and seek his fortune in New York City.

There was no Statue of Liberty to greet Edison as he came into New York Harbor by steamboat. The centennial of the country had not yet arrived. Many of today's landmarks were still undreamt of, but Wall Street and the New York Stock Exchange were already in place. It was there that Edison hoped to find investors for his inventions.

Later in an interview, Edison told the story of his first day. He arrived in the city starving and without a nickel in his pocket. Not one to beg, Edison tried to think of some other way to get his food. He saw a gentleman tasting a fine tea in a wholesale tea house. Going up to him, Edison inquired about the quality of the tea. The man gave him a tea bag to try for himself. Edison then walked to a restaurant and traded his tea for a five cent serving of apple dumplings and coffee. Edison said it was the best meal he ever had in his life.

After walking around this city of a million people for over a day, Edison found one of his telegrapher friends. Although he was out of work, too, the friend lent Edison a dollar. Edison then called on another telegraph friend, Franklin Pope, who worked at the Gold Indicator Company near Wall Street. Pope let Edison sleep on a cot in the cellar battery room as he continued to live on nickel meals.

Pope's job was to service a machine that telegraphed changing gold prices. It had been invented by Dr. Samuel Laws, who was taught electrical science by Joseph Henry. Edison studied this invention closely, and these studies would become useful shortly.

One day, the gold market was trading actively in great numbers when the central gold indicator device suddenly stopped transmitting. Hundreds of people from the gold broker offices came crowding into the company, surrounding Pope as he tried to fix the invention. Even Laws was summoned. In the chaos, Laws saw the ruin of his career and, according to Edison, became "the most excited person I had [ever] seen."

Edison saw that two gear wheels of the device were jammed by a broken metal spring. He told Laws that he had found the problem. "Fix it!" shouted Laws. Edison calmly removed the spring, reset the mechanism, and the instrument was soon working again. The very next day, Laws hired Edison to be his second telegraph expert, at a substantial salary.

After several months with the company, Edison started out on his own again. He created several telegraphic inventions that were sold to the Western Union Telegraph, the largest company in the electrical business. By 1871, Edison had filed for patents on 21 inventions. That same year he opened a manufacturing shop in Newark, New Jersey, to supply Western Union with 1,200 enhanced stock tickers. Soon several companies became interested in Edison's inventions.

Edison hired 50 employees to start production at his shop. Most of his skilled craftspeople had been clockmakers or machinists. There were few professional electricians at this time. Edison saved some of the top floor of the building for his laboratory.

Besides his inventions, one of Edison's female employees, Mary Stilwell, attracted his attention. Soon Edison was calling on her at the Sunday school where she taught class and taking her on carriage rides. Now that he was self-supporting, Edison considered getting married and starting a family. Although he often worked two or three shifts and slept on a cot in his shop, Edison thought about getting his own house, too.

Mary and Thomas were married on Christmas Day 1871. They had met, fallen in love, gotten engaged, gotten married, and obtained their first house, all in the same year. Time was always short for Edison.

By 1872 Edison had filed patents for 52 inventions, most of them on printing-telegraph improvements. In the next three years, Edison created inventions such as the electric pen and mimeograph for making copies of letters and the quadruplex telegraph. The quadruplex handled two messages simultaneously to and from each end of a telegraph line, making a total of four messages on a single wire. In 1875 Edison started working on a "harmonic telegraph" that would send multiple sound tones to allow for even more messages.

At the age of 29, in the centennial year of 1876, Edison opened his new laboratory on some land in the rural village of Menlo Park, New Jersey. He brought his most skilled craftspeople with him, including Charles Batchelor, John Kruesi, and a dozen others. From this time forward, the inventions for which Edison is best known began to appear.

Edison's first significant invention of this era was the improved telephone transmitter. The first telephone transmitter had been invented by Alexander Graham Bell and patented in early 1876. After two years of tests on 2,000 substances, Edison filed to patent the invention in February 1878.

Edison had learned that carbon granules were the key to the better sending of sound. Carbon was sensitive to pressure. With electricity added to the line, the carbon caused fluctuations in the circuit according to the sounds of the voice. It improved the loudness of sounds immensely.

The new telephone transmitter was an instant success. In the summer of 1878, there were 11,000 Bell telephones. When the Bell Telephone Company bought Edison's patent one year later, over 55,000 Edison telephones were already in service in 55 cities.

Edison's second significant invention of this time was the phonograph. While he and his staff tested the transmitter in 1877, Edison also tried to create a device to record telephone conversations. The instrument scratched sound vibrations on a disk or strip of paper. Early tests produced only faint sounds, but Edison was confident that he was on to a great invention.

Through the year, often working 20 hours a day, Edison tried various designs and materials. Then on December 4, Edison gave his newest sketch to John Kruesi, formerly a Swiss clockmaker. The drawing showed a roller covered with grooves. Two tubes, each with a membrane and needle attached, were positioned on each side of the roller. A crank and shaft were attached to the roller.

Kruesi set to work and had the model completed on December 6. When Edison told him it was a "talking machine," Kruesi thought he was joking.

Edison attached some tin foil around the cylinder and spoke into one of the tubes as he turned the crank. The needle vibrated to his voice and etched a wavy line in the foil. Then he rewound the cylinder to the starting point. Bringing the second tube into position, Edison spun the crank again. Other assistants gathered to see what would happen. The second needle followed the groove made by the first needle. Out of the invention came the sound of Edison's voice!

Everyone was astonished, and through the night, the whole crew took turns trying all sorts of songs and sounds.

On December 7, Edison took his invention to the editor of *Scientific American*. According the editor, Edison "turned a crank, and the machine inquired as to our health, asked how we liked the phonograph, informed us that *it* was very well, and bid us a cordial good night." Everyone in the office building came to see the new creation. Edison said, "They kept me at it until the crowd got so great that [the editor] was afraid the floor would collapse. The next morning the [news]papers contained columns."

Thomas Alva Edison, with his phonograph.
This photograph is by Mathew Brady.
(National Archives)

This talking machine, the phonograph, was Edison's first invention to get the attention of a wide public audience. While Bell was celebrated for the telephone, Edison was cheered for the "talking machine." He soon became known as the "Wizard of Menlo Park." But Edison wasn't finished with surprises yet.

Thomas Alva Edison

In September 1878, Edison chose the electric light as his next significant invention. Like the telegraph and telephone, Edison's light would not be the first, but it would be the best.

More than 20 experimenters had worked on electric lights before Edison. In the early 1700s, the English experimenter Francis Hauksbee had made a glass globe glow through the use of static electricity. In the early 1800s, Humphrey Davy had exhibited the first arc light—the light shined between two carbon rods connected to an early electric battery. Since 1838, others had tested lights similar to Edison's, with a glowing wire enclosed in a glass globe.

These early lights were rarely used because they were either too bright, too dim, too unreliable, too short-lived, or too expensive. Besides candles and oil lamps, the most popular form of lighting in the 1800s was gas lighting. Gas lighting was expensive as well as dangerous, especially if the flame was blown out and the gas left on to fill up a house or hotel.

Edison's electric lamp was the first to be cheap, long-lasting, and convenient, as well as the first to come with a complete electrical system so that it could be used in homes and offices.

Edison knew electric lamps would not be very useful without other inventions to support them and make them work. A vast electrical system to support lights in every home and office would need efficient electrical generators; central stations; distribution lines; meters, fuses, plugs, switches, sockets; and all sorts of other inventions. Edison decided to invent as many of these as he could, too.

After thousands of substances were tested over a great many hours by Edison and his staff, he felt ready to show off his new electric lamps. The lamps were emptied of air thanks to improved glass pumps so that the thin carbon wire inside would not burn up as they often had in old lights. The carbon wire, called a filament, glowed with light when electricity passed through it. The wire would burn up if exposed to the oxygen in the air. In the future, longer-lasting tungsten wire would be used as the filament. Edison considered tungsten but thought it was too expensive at the time.

The new lights were designed to exact electrical specifications so they would work well in a large system. They were made to operate on a low current so that copper wires supplying the electricity could be kept thin and cheap. Copper let electricity travel through it easily. More electricity could pass through large

The "Edison Effect" electric lamp. This was an early electron vacuum tube.
(Division of Electricity and Modern Physics, National Museum of American History, Smithsonian Institution, Negative no. 69,398)

amounts of copper, but that expense was unnecessary if the electrical devices only needed a little electricity.

After Christmas in 1879, Edison opened the laboratory to the public. The crowds increased day by day. On New Year's Eve, thousands of people came by train to see the show. At least 20 lights lit the way from the train station to the laboratory, with over 30 more shining brightly inside.

Enthusiastic newspaper articles soon appeared all over the world. Edison was well on his way to becoming the most famous American inventor of the century.

Along with all this invention activity, Thomas and Mary had three children. Marion, named after Tom's sister, was born in 1873, and Tom, Jr., was born in 1876. Edison nicknamed them Dot and Dash after the telegraph symbols. Then William was born in 1878. Like Edison had been when he was young, the children were brought up mostly by their mother; Edison spent almost all his time in the laboratory.

Young people all over the country were inspired by Edison's success. Many wanted to work for him for free. Edison took some of them on and paid them a salary after they proved they were good workers.

Edison continued to create inventions all his life. While most of his inventions involved the telegraph, phonograph, electric light, electrical systems, and electric batteries, he also invented a motion picture machine, fluorescent lamp, electric typewriter, electric locomotive, and an "Edison effect" lamp, which was the first electron vacuum tube. Some of these inventions took several years to perfect. For his electric storage battery project, begun in 1900, Edison devoted 10 years of effort, constantly trying to make the invention as efficient as possible.

For each success, Edison overcame a thousand failures. An essential component of his success was an optimistic attitude. "I never allow myself to become discouraged under any circumstances," Edison wrote in his autobiographical notes.

Other components included his imagination, his child-like love of life, and his persistence in obtaining his goals. A summary from one of the earliest writers on Edison's life, James Reid, said Edison was one of the simplest of men, careless in costume and fond of fun, having a highly inventive mind coupled with the playfulness of a child. One of Edison's interviewers, George Lathrop, said Edison's mind was open to every suggestion or idea, no matter how fanciful it seemed to others. "He never lets go of an idea," Lathrop wrote, "until he has tested all its possibilities."

At the age of 84, Thomas Alva Edison died on October 18, 1931. Considered one of the greatest Americans of his time, Edison contributed much to the future and left a legacy of inventions and ideas that are still in use today.

Chronology

February 11, 1847	Thomas Alva Edison is born in Milan, Ohio
1868	files for first invention patent
1871	marries Mary Stillwell. They eventually have three children
1877	Edison invents phonograph
1878	files for patent on telephone transmitter
1879	invents inexpensive, long-lasting light
1883	files first electronics patent on Edison Effect
1900	begins several years of effort improving his invention of the electric storage battery
October 18, 1931	dies in West Orange, New Jersey

Further Reading

Buranelli, Vincent. *Thomas Alva Edison*. Morristown, N.J.: Silver Burdett, 1989. A full-length biography written for young adults.

Greene, Carol. *Thomas Alva Edison: Bringer of Light*. Chicago: Children's Press, 1985. Biography written for young adults.

Guthridge, Sue. *Thomas A. Edison: Young Inventor*. New York: Macmillan, 1986. Part of the Childhood of Famous People series. Written for young adults.

Lampton, Christopher. *Thomas Alva Edison*. New York: Franklin Watts, 1988. A biography for young adults. Discusses Edison's contributions and the way in which electricity has altered the world. Includes a variety of illustrations.

Alexander Graham Bell
(1847–1922)

Alexander Graham Bell as a teenager.
(Library of Congress)

Alexander Graham Bell and his assistant Sumner Tainter adjusted their new equipment. They were in America's capital, Washington, D.C., in February 1880. Like the telephone, this invention used a sender and receiver. Unlike the telephone, this creation was without wires. Only open space stood between the two instruments.

The two inventors set up a series of lenses and mirrors, then took to their stations. Sumner stood at the sender. Bell readied the receiver. The sender's thin mirror vibrated as Sumner started to speak.

Sunshine came through the windows of their large laboratory. The sunbeams bounced off the mirrors and entered the lenses. The sunlight streaked across the space, creating a glowing cable of energy. Sumner laughed and sang a song.

Listening carefully at the receiver, a look of elation spread over Bell's face. Sumner's sounds resounded in his ear!

"I have heard articulate speech produced by sunlight!" Bell wrote of this occasion. "I have heard a ray of the sun laugh and cough and sing!"

Using the Greek word for light, Bell called his invention the *photo*phone. He considered it his greatest creation—the sending of speech across space by light!

Although he created several other inventions, the telephone is Bell's most widely known work. In the first century after its creation, hundreds of millions of telephones came into use. Their numbers continue to grow. Today, the people of almost 200 countries all over the world can be reached from any telephone in America. For a few coins, the entire system stands ready to send a message in a second to the home next door or across continents.

Alexander Bell was born on March 3, 1847, in the city of Edinburgh, Scotland. The day was the same as his grandfather's birthday.

Alexander's grandfather and father were speech teachers. Their first names were Alexander, too. They encouraged the Bell children to study everything related to speech.

Called Aleck as a boy, Bell had a brother Melly, short for Melville James, who was two years older. Younger brother Ted, whose given name was Edward Charles, came along a year after Aleck's birth.

Unlike his brothers, Aleck wasn't given a middle name. Although his father's middle name was Melville, Aleck was named Alexander Bell just like his grandfather. When he turned 11, his family accepted his choice of Graham for a second name. Aleck was impressed with Alexander Graham, a friend of the family who had recently visited them. When he grew up, Bell preferred to be called Graham.

Alexander Graham Bell

The earliest education for the Bell children came from their mother, Eliza Grace Symonds Bell. As well as the standard school subjects, she also gave them religious, drawing, and musical instruction. She had enjoyed a career as a portrait painter before starting her family. Although her hearing was weak, she also played the piano beautifully. Over time, Melly became the best student in reading and language, Ted the best artist, and Aleck the best musician.

Before their schooling started for the day, the boys also liked to have some fun. Through the window of their upper-floor room, they could see the young ladies that attended school in the house next door. Early in the morning, Aleck and Ted loved to stand at their window in their night clothes and make funny faces at the girls. The teacher had to put in thick glass to conceal the view so her students could study instead of giggle in class.

In 1857 Aleck and Ted began attending the nearby Hamilton Place Academy. In the following year, they joined Melly at the Royal High School. The school stood on Calton Hill with a view of the impressive Edinburgh Castle and Arthur's Seat, the lovely green hill by the sea said to have provided the view for the legendary King Arthur and his knights winning a contest against intruders.

The boys liked to hike about the countryside. "In boyhood," Bell later said, "I have spent many happy hours lying among the heather on the Scottish hills—breathing in the scenery around me with a quiet delight that is even now pleasant for me to remember." Aleck especially liked to sit on a high hill and dream about flight as he watched the birds wing their way above him.

Aleck enjoyed playing with Ben Herdman, a boy about the same age. They were having fun at Ben's father's mill one day when Aleck came up with his first invention. The father, John Herdman, said the boys could be useful if they would help him clean the husks off his grain. After some tiresome strokes with a nail brush, Aleck suggested that several brushes be installed on a paddle mechanism used at the mill. The grain could be cleaned as it was pushed through. Ben's father liked the idea, tried it, and it worked!

After his high school graduation, at the age of 15, Aleck left for London to visit his 72-year-old grandfather. Bell called this stay the turning point in his life.

Grandfather Bell gave Aleck the use of his library to study classic literature as well as writings on speech and sound. One of the articles that attracted Aleck's attention was titled "Principles of the Science of Tuning Instruments with Fixed Tones." The work was written by Lord Stanhope, the same man who helped Robert Fulton in his inventing career. This subject was one of the steps leading to the invention of the telephone.

Aleck returned to Edinburgh, in love with the science of speech and sound. To further encourage his children, his father offered a prize to Aleck and Melly if they could build a speaking machine.

The two boys accepted the challenge. They gathered some tin, rubber, cotton, iron wire, and other construction material and set to work. Aleck built the head, mouth, and tongue. Melly made the throat and vocal cords.

When the head was completed, the boys gave it a test. Out came the sound "Ma-ma"! Excited, the boys repeated the test over and over. Hearing the cries, a neighbor came to see what was the matter. She thought a baby was crying for its mother!

A short time after this occasion, Aleck's father, Alexander Melville Bell, completed the creation of a system of symbols he called Visible Speech. The symbols told how to use the vocal organs to say any sound exactly. The symbols were like a new alphabet for a universal language. A fellow speech scientist, Alexander Ellis, said alphabet science did not exist until Bell's system was created.

One set of symbols took care of every sound. Visible speech could be used to help people speak clearly, speak foreign languages, and even help the deaf to talk. They only needed to learn to use their vocal organs correctly.

Mr. Bell was soon appointed as a speech professor for the University of London. Melly took over his teaching duties in Edinburgh while Aleck became a teacher at an academy in Elgin, Scotland.

At this time, Aleck started to study the science of sound on his own. He discovered that when vowels were spoken, they made a musical tone that caused sympathetic vibrations outside the vocal cords, the vibrating tissues that create sound in the human voice. As he sang each vowel, he determined the exact pitch of the sound by holding a tuning fork in front of his mouth.

In March 1866, Aleck sent a letter describing his vowel tone discoveries to Alexander Ellis. Bell thought he was the first to learn about vowel tones, but Ellis informed him that the German scientist, Hermann von Helmholtz, had already written a book on this same subject.

Bell learned that Helmholtz used electromagnets in his studies, as well. Helmholtz used them to keep several tuning forks in constant vibration and create vowel sounds.

Alexander Graham Bell

With little knowledge of electricity, Bell thought that Helmholtz was also sending the vowel sounds along a telegraph line. This was not the case, but Bell's idea was another of his steps toward the concept of the telephone. Several steps still lay ahead, but his thoughts were on the correct course.

Ted wrote a letter to Aleck, discussing "[Aleck's] wish to do something great." Eventually, Aleck's wish came true but not soon enough for Ted to see. Ted made plans to be a teacher at the Elgin school, too, but fell ill with tuberculosis (TB). He weakened day by day. Aleck was at his bedside when he died in the spring of 1867.

In the following year, Aleck's father and uncle David traveled to the United States to give lectures on Visible Speech. Before returning from their tour, they also visited Canada to see some Scottish friends. Aleck's father was impressed with the climate and surroundings of the area.

Soon after their return, Melly showed signs of the same sickness that had taken Ted's life. Aleck tried to make things easier for his brother and took over some his teaching duties. For awhile, Melly seemed to be getting better. Then he took a turn for the worst and died in May 1870.

Now Aleck also began to feel the symptoms of TB. His father and mother were greatly concerned and thought a change of climate might help. Alexander Melville Bell wrote to his friends in Canada about bringing his family to live there.

In the summer of 1870, the Bells left London on a train and then took a steamship from the English coast. They arrived in Canada in August and settled in the town of Brantford, Ontario, within a few miles of their Scottish friends.

Graham, as Aleck now liked to be called, thought the end of his life was near. In the change of climate, however, he soon recovered. Graham started work as a teacher for the Boston School of Deaf Mutes in April 1871.

After a year of success at the school, Bell met Gardiner Hubbard. Besides being the head of the Clarke School for the Deaf, Hubbard was also a lawyer who handled patent cases. He was especially interested in telegraphy and other technical inventions.

Bell told him about a thought that had come to him when he was conducting his vowel tone tests. When he sang into the strings of a piano, the string that matched his note would vibrate in sympathy. Bell thought the vibrations of several strings could be sent along a single wire. At the end of the single wire would be a matching set of strings that would separately answer to each note. Each string could be attached to a telegraph set. Bell's idea was the harmonic telegraph.

Bell later learned that other inventors such as Thomas Edison and Elisha Gray were also working on similar projects. At the time, however, they hadn't created fully working models. There was still room for a newcomer.

Hubbard encouraged Bell to construct this invention. Thomas Sanders, the father of one of Bell's deaf students, offered funds for Bell's electrical experiments. Hubbard also gave support. They formed a partnership with Bell for an equal share in future profits.

Bell still needed to support himself with housing, food, and clothing while he conducted his experiments. At this stage of events, he was often short of funds. As well as a part-time professorship at Boston University, Bell also accepted some deaf students for individual private lessons. He gave instruction to five-year-old George Sanders and Mabel Hubbard, Gardiner's teenage daughter.

Besides the harmonic telegraph, Bell also worked on a phonautograph. This invention drew the vibrations of sounds. Bell noticed how the sounds were drawn in the shape of bouncing wavy lines. When completed, Bell's deaf students would be able to see the shape of a sound so they could learn to speak clearly. Bell also thought these shapes could be included in the Visible Speech textbook.

The wavy lines created by speech were interesting when one considered the theory that sound is a wave that moves parts of the ear that the brain then senses and translates into meaning. Bell was fascinated with the way the tiny, thin eardrum set the larger bones of the inner ear in motion. Bell's tests eventually gave him the idea for an eardrumlike telephone that would set a fluctuating electric current in motion.

Solving all the issues that sprang up with the harmonic telegraph and his early telephone proved to be a hard task for Bell. Although he had a great knowledge of speech, he had little knowledge of electricity. To add to his challenge was the lack of support—some people said he was foolishly wasting his time.

In March 1875, Bell visited scientist Joseph Henry. Henry was now the director of the Smithsonian Institution in Washington, D.C. Celebrated for his electrical work since the early telegraph and electromagnet days, Henry was now nearly 80 years old.

Alexander Graham Bell

Bell explained his idea of sending speech by telegraph. Henry thought Bell's concept was the seed of a great invention. When Bell said that he lacked the electrical knowledge to succeed, Henry said, *"Get it!"*

"I cannot tell you how much these two words have encouraged me," wrote Bell after his visit. Like Samuel Morse, Alexander Graham Bell was helped by Joseph Henry. Although he was a teacher, Bell chose to conquer the fields of invention and electrical science, too. "Morse conquered his electrical difficulties although he was . . . a painter, and I don't intend to give in either," wrote Bell.

Nearly all the top electrical experimenters in the Boston area made use of the shop owned by Charles Williams. Here, electrical equipment could be made to order. Thomas Watson was one of the workers employed at the shop.

Thomas Watson began working on assignment for Bell in 1875. Although they first started with the harmonic telegraph, they soon turned their efforts toward the telephone. On June 2, after several weeks of tests, the two experimenters obtained their first success.

When one of the telegraph receivers failed to sound, Watson plucked at the strip of metal that stood over the telegraph's electromagnet. Bell heard the twanging sound come out of the telegraph set on his end. Greatly excited, Bell rushed over to Watson to tell him the good news. They had first-hand evidence that electric current that could carry fluctuations, or wavelike changes, in sound.

Bell came up with a membrane design for the telephone, like a large eardrum, that Thomas Watson then built. "At last," Bell wrote, "a means has been found which will render possible the transmission . . . of the human voice."

About this time, Bell became aware of his growing love for his student, Mabel Hubbard. Deaf since the age of five from scarlet fever, Mabel was an intelligent girl who was skilled in lip-reading and speech. They became engaged on her 18th birthday on Thanksgiving Day in 1875.

On January 12, 1876, Bell was at the Hubbard house, working into the evening. He was trying to complete the papers for his telephone patent to give to Gardiner Hubbard. Bell often worked late, and Mabel teased him about his "night owl" habits. As midnight came, he was still writing in their library.

Mabel called to him from the top of the stairway to not stay up so late. Bell came running up the stairs and asked her to let him keep working since he was so close to completing the telephone specifications. As he continued to work, she said she was going to paint his portrait. She later gave it to him. It was a good likeness, of his habits. The canvas contained the image of a great white owl.

Gardiner Hubbard filed for the American telephone patent on Valentine's Day. On his birthday of March 3, Bell's patent was approved.

One of the earliest Bell telephones. A drawing of a design similar to this one can be seen in figure seven of his first telephone patent.
(Division of Electricity and Modern Physics, National Museum of American History, Smithsonian Institution, Negative no. 28,421)

The approval came none too soon. On January 14, Thomas Edison had filed a warning notice, called a caveat, with the Patent Office that stated he was working on a harmonic telegraph that used a moving membrane to emit sounds. Elisha Gray had submitted his notice describing a telephone on February 14, the same day that Bell's patent was filed.

Fortunately for Bell, these notices only said they were *trying* to make these devices, not that they had succeeded. They failed to file for actual patents in time to be first.

Bell wanted to show that his telephone was not only the first but also the best. "I am sure of fame, fortune, and success if I can only persevere in *perfecting* my apparatus," Bell wrote. He learned that a German inventor, Philipp Reis, had succeeded in making a telephone emit the tones of spoken sounds. Bell knew that his invention was better, however, since it could carry the full quality of speech and conversation.

Within a week of the patent's approval, on March 10, Watson and Bell gained a sample of what Bell's telephone could do. Bell had a needle connected to the bottom of the telephone's transmitting membrane and a small cup of water placed underneath. One wire connected to the needle and a second wire to the metal cup. The electric current would change as the spoken words moved the needle up and down in the cup. By adding sulfuric acid to the water, the signal would be strong enough to send sounds. Along with other specific chemicals, sulfuric acid had been found helpful in conducting electricity through chemical action. To increase the signal still further, the transmitter was connected to a galvanic battery (open at the top so electricity-generating chemicals could be added if needed).

According to Thomas Watson's autobiography, *Exploring Life*, Bell spilled some battery acid on his clothes. Watson was in another room listening for sounds on the receiving end of the telephone when suddenly the words, "Mr. Watson, come here, I want you!" came to his ears. Watson wrote, "The transmission of this first sentence was so impressive that I noted it in my diary." Watson rushed to see Bell. Watson wrote of Bell's excitement at learning that the telephone worked so well, "He forgot the incident [the spill] in his joy over the success of the new transmitter." Bell then exchanged places with Watson. According to Bell's laboratory notes, he had trouble understanding some of Watson's words at first, then Bell noted, "the sentence 'Mr. Bell do you understand what I say?' . . . came quite clearly and intelligibly." Bell wrote about the event two days later without mentioning the accident with the acid. In these notes, Bell recorded the full sentence of what he shouted to Watson as, "Mr. Watson—come here—I want to see you."

In June 1876, Bell displayed the telephone at the United States Centennial Exhibition in Philadelphia. The Centennial was created to show how far the young United States had come in the 100 years since its birth. It was built to surpass the greatest exhibitions of Europe, including England's Crystal Palace and France's Exposition Universelle.

All the major countries of the world participated. As well as exhibitions for new electrical and mechanical devices, there were buildings for education, science, art, and agriculture. There was also a Women's Pavilion where Exhibit 202 contained a sketch by Mabel Hubbard.

On June 25, Bell operated his telephone for the exhibition judges. They were impressed. The emperor of Brazil exclaimed in surprise when he first heard words on the telephone. Sir William Thomson, a respected English scientist who later became Lord Kelvin, said that the telephone was the most wonderful thing he had seen in America.

Bell and Watson designed two types of telephones. In one, the voice alone induced an electric current. The second one used a battery to supply the electric signal. At first, they concentrated their efforts on the voice-activated type. In October, Watson and Bell had their first telephone conversation without changing places. They sent and received sentences using the same thin steel transmitting instruments at each end.

In April 1877, the first telephone service was set in operation between the electrical shop of Charles Williams and his home. The growth of the telephone business started to expand at an ever increasing rate. Graham Bell was a success!

On July 11, Graham and Mabel were married. As a symbol of his love, Graham gave almost all his 1,507 shares of Bell Telephone Company stock to Mabel as a wedding gift. He kept only a token 10 shares for himself.

Other inventors were surprised at themselves for not being the first to create a conversation-carrying telephone. In late 1877, Bell felt the same feeling when he heard that Edison had invented the phonograph.

"It is a most astonishing thing to me," said Bell, "that I could possibly have let this invention slip through my fingers."

Edison also contributed to the telephone by his invention of a carbon transmitter that he patented in 1878. Edison had focused on the type of telephone that used an electric battery. In 1879, the Bell Telephone Company bought the rights to Edison's patent, and their company quickly started to grow. In the summer of 1878, there were 11,000 Bell telephones in service. Three years later, according to their annual report, there were 132,692.

Lawsuits to get a piece of the telephone business started to increase. Over time, 600 lawsuits were filed. All the cases ended in Bell's favor, except for two minor ones. Although others claimed to be first, Bell was shown to be the true inventor every time.

Except for the legal cases, Bell essentially retired from the telephone business after a few years. He bought a home in Washington, D.C. and a summer home in Nova Scotia, Canada. Bell devoted his time to studies of science, inventions, and the deaf.

In 1881, the year after he created the photophone, Bell invented an electric metal detector called the telephonic bullet probe. Bell used the instrument to try to locate the bullet that lodged in President James Garfield's body when he was assassinated.

In that same year, Bell also invented the "vacuum jacket" after his newborn son Edward died of lung failure. This invention tried to provide artificial breathing for an ill person, much like later iron lung equipment did, by altering air pressure to the chest at regular intervals. Graham and Mabel also had two daughters, Elsie and Marion, who grew up to maturity, and one other son, Robert, who lived only a short time like his brother.

From 1881 to 1885, Sumner Tainter, Bell, and Bell's cousin Chester Bell created the wax phonograph. Their efforts led to improvements in Thomas Edison's tin foil invention in the way that Edison's transmitter had helped the telephone.

Bell also continued to work with the deaf. In 1887, the parents of a six-year-old girl who was blind as well as deaf consulted with Bell. He referred them to the head of an institution for the blind who in turn recommended Annie Sullivan to be the young girl's teacher. Sullivan became known as a miracle worker for teaching the girl to speak. The young girl, Helen Keller, became famous. As she grew up, she came to visit Graham Bell several times. She expressed her gratitude to him in the beginning of her book *The Story of My Life.*

After studying the census counts of the deaf, Bell conceived of a census card sorting invention in 1889. Then he learned that Herman Hollerith was already ahead of him with an electrical data processing invention that also sorted cards. Impressed with Hollerith's design, Bell chose not to continue efforts in this area.

In the 1890s Bell started to work on "flying machine" experiments. Bell tested gunpowder rockets, giant kites, model helicopters, and wing designs. His friend Samuel Langley successfully flew engine-powered, unmanned airplanes hundreds of feet into the sky. Langley's work, often performed in the company of the supportive Bell, inspired the Wright Brothers who successfully flew the first manned engine-powered airplane.

In 1902, at the age of 55, Bell invented a new design based on his kite experiments. "A figure composed of four equilateral triangles having four triangular faces bounded by six equal edges . . . a

Alexander Graham Bell, seated with Helen Keller, and Annie Sullivan standing behind.
(Library of Congress)

new form of architecture"—Bell patented this tetrahedral design in 1904.

This architecture was used in the 20th century to construct the dome-shaped structures designed by Buckminster Fuller, who independently conceived of this design. Bell created a tall tetrahedral tower using lightweight steel pipes. In 1907, one of his giant kites composed of this architecture carried a man high in the sky.

In spite of Bell's efforts in other areas, his telephone outshined all his other inventions. The telephone continued to be improved. "The telephone reminds me of a child only it grows much more rapidly," wrote Bell. Telephones became the end points of a complex system of switchboards and wires. One of the inventors of improved switchboards was George Westinghouse. Soon there were hundreds of inventors trying to improve each segment of the system.

At the age of 75, Alexander Graham Bell died on August 2, 1922, at his summer home. The telephone lived on.

At the Centennial in 1876, one telephone set was in operation. By the United States Bicentennial in 1976, 150 million telephones were in service in America. One of Bell's biographers, Herbert Casson, wrote, the telephone is now "in most places taken for granted, as though it were a part of the natural phenomena of this planet."

Like other great inventions, the telephone started from simple beginnings but its future is open to the imagination. As Casson wrote, "Guesses as to the future of the telephone may fall short of what the reality will be . . . When Bell stood in a dingy workshop in Boston and heard the clang . . . come over an electric wire, who could have foreseen the massive structure of the Bell System, built up by [over] half the telephones of the world . . . ?"

Chronology

March 3, 1847	Alexander Bell is born in Edinburgh, Scotland
1871	teaches deaf students at Boston School
1875	hears first proof of electricity's ability to carry sound fluctuations
1876	files for telephone patent; hears first sentences spoken on telephone
1880	Bell invents photophone
1881	invents telephonic bullet probe and vacuum jacket
1902	invents tetrahedral architecture
August 2, 1922	dies at summer home near Baddeck, Nova Scotia, in Canada. Bell's request for the words *citizen of the United States* on his epitaph is fulfilled

Further Reading

Bruce, Robert V. *Bell: Alexander Graham Bell and the Conquest of Solitude.* Boston: Little, Brown and Company, 1973. A thorough, well-researched biography of Bell. Informative.

Davidson, Margaret. *The Story of Alexander Graham Bell: Inventor of the Telephone.* New York: Dell, 1989. Written for young adults.

Eber, Dorothy Harley. *Genius At Work: Images of Alexander Graham Bell.* New York: Viking Press, 1982. Filled with interesting photographs of Bell's Nova Scotia summers. Includes photographs of Bell's tetrahedral structures.

Pelta, Kathy. *Alexander Graham Bell.* Morristown, N.J.: Silver Burdett Press, 1989. A full-length biography for young adults.

Herman Hollerith
(1860–1929)

Herman Hollerith as a young man.
(Library of Congress)

*E*ver since the earliest civilizations, leaders have wanted to know the size and value of their lands. They have asked questions that required numerical answers: What is the population of the country? How many cattle and other livestock are there? How many crops and crafted goods are produced? The answers were always counted by hand. One by one, the numbers were tallied, often with beads, stones, or notches on wood or clay tablets.

Hand methods were cumbersome but workable when the numbers were small. By 1880, however, the numbers were very great. The population of the United States was thought to be over 50 million people and the population of the world one billion. Counting by hand took too long.

In the 1880 U.S. Census, people were asked several questions on topics such as their age, gender, education, country of birth, and so on. The total number of census answers for the country came to well over a billion. Just to say the words from one to a billion, averaging three seconds each, would take someone, working eight hours every day without a break, over 285 years. The time to count and record the answers would take even longer.

Incredibly, America and the entire world were still trying to count by hand when Herman Hollerith came along.

In 1889, Hollerith brought his electric data processing invention to the U.S. Census Office in Washington, D.C., for a contest. He would be competing against two hand counting systems, one conceived by Charles Pidgin and the other by William Hunt. The winner would be awarded the contract for the 1890 Census.

The goal of the contest was to process census count information for the city of St. Louis in the shortest possible time.

The first step was simply to record the information. Pidgin's team of clerks would be using various colored inks on slips of paper. Hunt's clerks would write their information on colored cards. Hollerith's group would use his keyboard punch invention to create round holes in specific areas on large blank cards.

The contest started. Clacking and scribbling sounds filled the air. Seventy-two hours and 27 minutes later, Hollerith's group completed the task. The Hunt and Pidgin teams continued to scratch away. After 110 hours and 56 minutes, Pidgin's clerks were done. After 144 hours and 25 minutes, the Hunt team finally finished.

Hollerith won, but the test was only halfway through. Now the data needed to be sorted and summed. With the color-coded paper and cards, the clerks working for Hunt and Pidgin could easily hand sort the information into groups for the swift totaling of the figures. For this task, Hollerith introduced his electric tabulating machine.

Herman Hollerith

The second segment of the contest began. This test was completed in less time than the first. Hunt's totals were finished in 55 hours and 22 minutes, and Pidgin's in 44 hours and 41 minutes.

Hollerith's equipment completed the same task in only five hours and 28 minutes. His creation added the totals 10 times faster than Hunt's system and eight times faster than Pidgin's. Herman Hollerith had just introduced the first successful electric data processing invention.

Herman Hollerith was born to Johann and Franciska Hollerith in the leap year of 1860, on February 29, in Buffalo, New York. He was the seventh and youngest child of the family. His mother's family, the Brunns, who had come from Europe, owned a factory in Buffalo with a reputation for building well-designed and beautiful horse carriages. Johann Hollerith had been a professor of languages in Germany before he emigrated to America. He now earned income from his ownership of some Midwest farmland.

"Paddle your own canoe" were the words of advice that Johann gave to his children. By this, he meant that they should take control of their own life. When Herman was only nine and his brother George 14, their father died from a horse carriage accident. Shortly afterward, their mother moved the children to New York City where she could earn a living making women's hats.

Around this time, Herman showed signs of rebellion at school. He slipped out of class when the time for spelling lessons came. One time the teacher locked the door. So young Hollerith jumped out of the window, from the second floor! Although he learned to like arithmetic and numbers, Hollerith was sensitive about his spelling skills all his life.

Aided by tutoring from a friendly church minister, Herman improved his education to a great extent. At 12, he passed all the exams for acceptance to the New York City College. It was then common for college-bound students to take entrance exams at an early age. He attended the college from the autumn of 1872 to 1875. At 15, his scores placed him in the top 14 out of 108 students in his class.

Then he entered the Columbia College School of Mines where he received high grades in several courses, including geometry, graphics, engineering, and surveying. The fatherless teenager

Herman Hollerith at age nine.
(Library of Congress)

became good friends with some of his professors, especially William Trowbridge, the head of the engineering department.

Shortly after graduation in 1879, Hollerith was invited by Professor Trowbridge to work at the U.S. Government Census Office in Washington, D.C. There were more than 1,500 employees in that office. Besides the Population Division, there were other divisions in the Census Office for special census categories.

Trowbridge was called their expert special agent in charge of statistics (numerical information) on the power and machinery used at companies across the nation. Hollerith accepted the assignment of collecting statistics on the steam and water power used in iron and steel making.

At the Census Office, Hollerith also became acquainted with Dr. John Shaw Billings. He was in charge of census health statistics while also employed as an army surgeon. He eventually became a full professor at the University of Pennsylvania and organizer of the great New York Public Library. He also gave Herman Hollerith the idea for his invention.

On a summer evening in 1881, Hollerith attended a dance at the Potomac Boat Club, of which he was a member. His young dance partner, Kate Billings, later asked her mother to invite him to their home for Sunday supper.

Kate's father, the same Dr. John Shaw Billings, stayed for the Sunday supper and was soon talking shop with Hollerith. They talked about the years of effort involved in completing a census by hand.

"He said to me there ought to be a machine for doing the purely mechanical work of tabulating population and similar statistics," Hollerith wrote later in a letter. Tabulating meant calculating group totals and entering them into number tables. Billings's idea inspired Hollerith to invent such a machine.

Soon after the Sunday supper, Hollerith returned to the Census Office and talked with the head of the Population Division. He gained his approval to work as a clerk to see how the slow counting by hand was performed. After careful study, Hollerith started to create his electric counting invention.

Kate Billings said later, "I remember the first little wooden model which Herman Hollerith brought to our library many evenings while they were puzzling their brains over its adaptation. Father had no mechanical gifts—so the entire credit is Mr. Hollerith's."

Hollerith grew excited with the fun of inventing. Apparently whatever ideas young Kate and Herman had for each other were overwhelmed by his enthusiasm for creating something new. She eventually married someone else.

After Hollerith came up with a design, he thought about forming an enterprise to make the invention. He asked Dr. Billings to be his business partner. Billings turned Hollerith down. His interest extended only to the wish that a census solution be found.

Without significant financial support or business partners, Hollerith was on his own to create the machine. He would have to continue working at a day job while he tested his invention ideas in his spare time.

The funds for the 1880 Census were swiftly vanishing due to the extensive labor costs required. Before the end of 1881, the census experts started returning to their teaching careers. After similar encouragement, Hollerith became an engineering teacher at the Massachusetts Institute of Technology in the autumn of 1882.

While employed at the school, Hollerith found time to experiment on his invention. As his creation took form, he thought about learning how to get a patent. He chose to continue a career habit he had started early in life.

As a student of mining engineering at the Columbia College School of Mines, Hollerith had spent his summer vacation working in northern Michigan mines. As a possible inventor of census equipment, Hollerith had worked for the Census Office in Washington, D.C. Now as an inventor seeking to know about patents, he took what seemed the next logical step. In 1883, Hollerith returned to Washington to become an assistant in the Patent Office. As an examiner, Hollerith saw thousands of patent filings. He soon became an expert in their composition as well as the requirements for their approval.

After he mastered the patent procedures, Hollerith opened his own office as an "Expert and Solicitor of Patents" in the spring of 1884. Now Hollerith felt ready to file his own patents.

On September 23, 1884, Hollerith filed for the first patent on his electrical counting invention. Since the summer of 1881, Hollerith had been considering and testing the features of his invention. Gradually, the creation had begun to take form.

At first, Hollerith had visualized using long paper strips to record all the census information. Each individual's answers would go on a section of the strip. Holes would be punched in certain spots if the individual was female, male, old, young, and so on. Each strip could have information on thousands of people.

Then the strip would be run over a roller that made electrical contacts through the holes to move electromechanical counters. Battery-powered, the device would operate as an automatic feed, like the automatic telegraphs that Thomas Edison worked on years earlier. The mechanism would move the strip along from its beginning to the end.

The counters would first be set to zero. When a specific hole was found, a corresponding counter would move forward one position. There would be a separate counter for each census answer such as age group by gender, education level, and so on.

The concept was fine except for one major issue. It was very difficult to find individual information in strips of paper hundreds of feet long.

Hollerith recalled a train ride where the conductor punched some holes in his train ticket. Certain sections of the ticket signified his height, hair color, and other characteristics. The conductor wanted to be sure that each passenger was identified and held his or her own ticket.

In like fashion, Hollerith decided each individual counted in the census would get his or her own card or ticket. He changed his invention to handle a tall stack of individually numbered cards instead of a single long strip.

In the future, electronic computers would go through similar stages. Paper tape readers, card readers, and magnetic tape drives would be used as input and recording devices.

Having designed his census inventions, but still short on money to go into business, Hollerith had to find something else to do. In the Patent Office, Hollerith had seen that a great number of invention applications described devices for the ever-expanding railroads. These companies were well financed and could afford to support inventions useful to the railroads. Hollerith thought that he could invent something to improve railroad equipment such as air brakes like those of George Westinghouse.

By the summer of 1885, Hollerith was in St. Louis, Missouri, where he was soon working for the Mallinckrodt Brake Company. John Mallinckrodt was a former Westinghouse air brake repairman who had formed his own company. In January 1886, the inventive Hollerith was issued three patents for his design of new electrical railway car brakes.

When a train equipped with Westinghouse air brakes stopped, it took a few seconds for the compressed air to travel through the air hoses to every car in the train. The rear cars would bump into the cars that stopped first. With electricity traveling the same distance in a split second, all the cars of a train could be signaled to stop at the same time. Hollerith also made the braking pressure adjustable so that just the right amount of force would be applied.

Hollerith attended the 1887 train brake contests in Burlington, Iowa. He and J. Carpenter formed a team to compete against the companies of Westinghouse, Card, and the American Brake Co.

The Carpenter-Hollerith brakes performed so well that the Westinghouse team had to scramble to improve their test times. It is said by Hollerith's family that Westinghouse offered to buy

Hollerith's brake patents, as Westinghouse usually did when faced with advanced inventions. Hollerith declined the offer because he hoped to go into business against the Westinghouse Company after the contests. However, Hollerith found he lacked the finances to compete successfully. The improved Westinghouse brakes soon became the industry standard.

However, in 1887, Hollerith did gain his first census customer. He set up his electric tabulating invention for the city of Baltimore, Maryland. The machine was fast, but creating the cards was slow. Using a train conductor's device, Hollerith punched thousands of stiff cards by hand. "I punched down one side, across the bottom and then up the other side," Hollerith recalled in a letter written years later.

After a few days of punching, Hollerith's hand and arm ached. He continued to work, however, since he wanted to succeed. Eventually, this effort gave him the inspiration to invent a keyboard device that would punch a card's holes with an easy touch of the hand. He also added a "gang punch" invention that took care of several cards at a time.

The tests in Baltimore went well and soon other cities expressed their interest. In October 1888, Hollerith went to Boston and visited the former electrical shop of Charles Williams (owned by the Western Electric Company since 1882) to see the employees make his newest electric data processing machine. This shop, once used by Thomas Edison and Alexander Graham Bell, still continued to construct equipment for electrical experimenters.

After his return to Washington, Hollerith began courting the educated and pretty Lucia Talcott. Her mother was impressed with Hollerith. In November 1888, she wrote, "He has a fine education and more than average ability and no end of perseverance . . . He has staked everything—all his money, his time and his thoughts—upon this invention, and it would be a terrible disappointment to him if it failed."

In 1889, the contest to win the United States 1890 Census contract was a success for Hollerith. He was also awarded a gold medal at the Paris Exposition Universelle of 1889, and the Franklin Institute in America gave him a medal in February 1890.

After all the census information was collected, Hollerith's electrical equipment began operation for the U.S. Census Office on July 1, 1890. To further improve its performance, Hollerith added his invention of a sorting box to collect the cards after they were counted. Instead of being collected at random, the cards would be

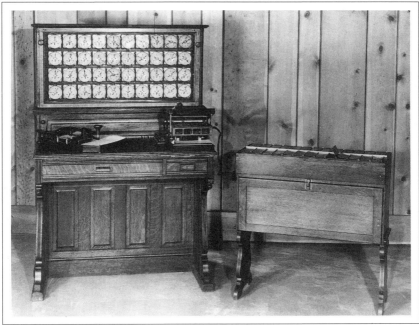

Hollerith's early electric data processing inventions. The tabulating machine on the left automatically counted census numbers according to specific card codes. The left side device on the desk top is a pantograph punch, used for making the card holes. The device on the right side of the desk top is where cards are entered for processing. When the metal pins reach through the holes of each card, they connect electrical circuits, activating specific counter dials. The machine on the right sorted the cards.
(IBM Archives, International Business Machines)

stacked into groups. These stacks made second runs easier to obtain further information.

In mid-August, just six weeks after starting, Hollerith's electrical counting machines reported a U.S. population of 62.5 million. In a task that used to take years, the entire country had been counted. Then the census workers sorted the census cards into new combinations, giving them information they never had time to create before.

On September 15, 1890, Herman and Lucia were married. They eventually had six children—Lucia, Nannie, Virginia, Herman,

Richard, and Charles. Herman built a workshop for his family, and some of the children grew up to become inventors, too.

In the next 10 years, the electric data processing machines were used for the censuses of Austria, Canada, Norway, France, Italy, Russia, and Germany. Hollerith soon realized his inventions could be used in businesses, too. He formed his own company that began constructing copies of his creations. Insurance, railroad, and many other companies became his customers.

In 1901, Hollerith added the automatic card feed and automatic sorting machine to his list of inventions. He obtained nearly 40 American patents over time.

In 1911, at the age of 51, Hollerith sold his Tabulating Machine Company to the newly formed Computing-Tabulating- Recording Company. This company continued to grow and expand its business all over the world. In 1924, the company changed its name to International Business Machines, better known as IBM.

Hollerith had a special strategy that enabled his electric counting business to become successful. Instead of selling his machines, Herman kept ownership and rented them out to others. This idea provided steady income and growth for his company.

Following the same strategy, International Business Machines and American Telephone & Telegraph became the giants of their industries in the 20th century. Some of Hollerith's associates and employees became top executives in these two companies.

When his early inventions first became successful, Hollerith set a new goal for himself in 1895. "If I could only have enough money," he wrote, "I could lead a pleasant life and be quite proud." When he sold his company 16 years later, Hollerith was given more than $1.2 million for his share. For a man who started as a census employee with a salary of $600 a year, this was a very substantial sum.

Hollerith enjoyed the pleasant life in a custom-built house on some Virginia farmland overlooking the Chesapeake and East rivers. He also built a second house on three acres of land in Washington, D.C., for social occasions. Living to age 69, Hollerith died in Washington, D.C., on November 15, 1929.

Herman Hollerith's inventions marked the birth of the data processing industry. IBM continued to offer business machines based on Hollerith's ideas. Hollerith's equipment and cards became a common sight in offices around the world.

Over time, Hollerith's inventions were improved with additional mechanical and electrical changes. Then, in the late 1930s, under the guidance of Howard Aiken of Harvard University, IBM's Hollerith-inspired devices were combined with the concepts of Charles Babbage to make the first electrical computer.

Charles Babbage was an English inventor and mathematician who had designed a machine called the analytical engine in the 1830s, a century earlier. The machine was supposed to accept cards as input, store instructions on cards, calculate, make decisions, and report the results, but Babbage was never able to complete his invention.

Howard Aiken and his team of inventors were more successful. Completed in 1944, the combination was called the Mark I, an invention that started the computer era. Soon, electronic computers, filled with Edison-inspired electron vacuum tubes, began taking over the data processing field in the mid-20th century.

All this time, Hollerith cards were still used to enter data and information into the computers. The cards were the size of 1889 dollar bills and had their holes in the same arrangements just like the cards Hollerith had designed years earlier. Eventually, substitutes were invented. In the final quarter of the 20th century, portable disks and electric typewriter keyboards replaced the cards and card equipment.

The basics of Hollerith's system still survive. Just like his early machines, today's computers still give out useful information through electrical processing. Also, just as Hollerith expanded the services of his invention to other industries, computer uses have continued to expand in incredible ways.

Computers can be trained, or programmed, to do an almost unlimited number of tasks. All the fields of the inventors in this book have been touched by computers. Transportation, agriculture, long-distance communication, material development, electrical systems, transportation safety, telephones, and many other areas are served by computers all across the country.

It all started with an inventor. Herman Hollerith saw a task that could be improved, studied the situation, and came up with a solution. Then he continued to improve his invention until it became successful. A success that was confirmed by the census superintendent of the time, Robert Porter, who gladly announced in 1890, "For the first time in the history of the world, the count of the population of a great nation has been made with the help of electricity."

Chronology

February 29, 1860	Herman Hollerith is born in Buffalo, New York
1884	files first patent on electrical counting invention
1886	receives three patents on electrical railway car brakes
1889	wins contract to use electric data processing machines for United States Census; is awarded gold medal at Paris Exposition Universelle
1901	receives patents on automatic card feed and automatic sorting inventions
1911	sells his Tabulating Machine Company to Computing-Tabulating-Recording Company (later IBM)
November 15, 1929	dies in Washington, D.C.

Further Reading

Austrian, Geoffrey D. *Herman Hollerith : Forgotten Giant of Information Processing.* New York: Columbia University Press, 1982. Well-researched biography. Informative.

Hollerith, Virginia. *ISIS.* Vol. 62, Part 1, No. 211, Spring 1971. "Biographical Sketch of Herman Hollerith." pp. 69–78. Washington, D.C.: The Smithsonian Institution. Written by daughter of Herman Hollerith. Short but informative.

Index

Bold numbers indicate main headings

Index

Index

Index

Index